ISBN: 1524-2269

0 0 1 2 3 4 5 6 7 8 9 0 0

Imagining Psychological Life:
Philosophical, Psychological, and Poetic
Reflections

Festschrift in Honor of
Robert D. Romanyshyn

Introduction
Stephen Aizenstat, Ph.D.

Editor's Introduction
Michael P. Sipiora, Ph.D.

Philosophical Psychology Series

Edited by
Brent Dean Robbins

Trivium Publications
Pittsburgh, PA

Table of Contents

8

Table of Contents

Introduction

Stephen Aizenstat, Ph.D.
Pacifica Graduate Institute's Chancellor and Founding President

The dream of Pacifica began revealing herself in the late 1970's and early 1980's when there were just a few of us here in Santa Barbara who heard the call. I remember asking James Hillman: "Who might we bring to Pacifica to offer cutting edge thinking in the fields of Phenomenology and Depth/Archetypal Psychology?" One name immediately rose to the top of the list: Dr. Robert Romanyshyn. Robert was, above all others, the person who could help build the foundation that would secure and support this radical initiative in education. At that time Dr. Romanyshyn was teaching and conducting research at the University of Dallas and had a distinguished body of work already to his credit. It was clear to us that his vision and mastery of scholarship was rooted in the very soil that gave sustenance to Pacifica's dream of a soul-centered school of depth psychological study. The addition of Robert to the faculty marked the emergence of Pacifica Graduate Institute as a premier school of depth psychology.

Dr. Romanyshyn first taught at Pacifica in 1985 when the current doctoral programs in Depth Psychology were just beginning to emerge. He became a Core faculty member in 1991 and has exerted a formative influence that remains a vital part of the institution today and will for years to come. So many of us—faculty, staff, students, and Board members— have all been deeply touched by his keen intellect, his artistry as a lecturer, the poetics of his imagination, and, too, his profound dedication to mission and vision. Robert is indeed a charismatic teacher. Literally thousands of students in both graduate studies and public programs have been inspired by the deep reflection and the animated presence alive in his classroom presentations and professional lectures. His flair for dramatic enactments continues to bring students into dynamic encounters with the soul.

Perhaps the true measure of a person is their legacy. Robert is mentor to countless students many of whom have gone on to distinguished academic careers. Many more have become highly skilled, successful clinicians. Indeed, he did more than train therapists, although he did train students in a remarkable level of clinical sophistication that came from his own extensive background as a clinical psychologist.

He educated psychologists in the history, thought, and language of the psyche. Robert cultivated his students' capacity to serve in the making of soul in both the classroom and the consulting room.

Dr. Romanyshyn's numerous publications helped Pacifica Graduate Institute establish itself as a leading center of depth psychology in the United States. His first book, *Psychological Life: From Science to Metaphor* (1982), gave voice to a sophisticated, imaginative vision of phenomenological psychology. *Technology as Symptom and Dream* (1989), his second book which is in its sixth reprinting, has been widely praised as a work that makes an original and important contribution toward an understanding of the soul of technology. *The Soul in Grief: Love, Death and Transformation* (1999), a profound reflection that has made a difference in so many people's lives, was followed by a revised second edition of his first book with new material and re-titled as *Mirror and Metaphor: Images and Stories of Psychological Life* (2000). A dozen of his provocative and inspiring essays were collected in a volume entitled *Ways of the Heart: Essays Toward an Imaginal Psychology* (2001). *The Wounded Researcher* (2007) makes a definitive contribution to the field by identifying and incorporating the unconscious dynamic active in the research process. In addition are the over 60 book chapters and journal articles within a list of achievements that continue to grow. Robert's work has also been the subject of internet and radio interviews, and television programs. His provocative presentations have stirred audiences across the U.S., Canada, Europe, Africa, New Zealand and Australia. Underpinning all that he has accomplished in print and presentation is one thing: his dedication to the integrity and discipline of reflective thought and poetic reverie.

It would be hard to overemphasize the unique role that Robert has played in developing our research courses. As it emerged as an academic institution, the research dimension of Pacifica Graduate Institute was crucial to its on-going mission and vision, specifically the integrity of its academic status and the vitality of its educational processes. Robert was asked to develop a model for research that answered to Pacifica's calling as a place for developing depth and its motto of serving the soul of the world. He responded by creating a human science research model that incorporated a variety of qualitative methods. Research, in this model, is profoundly interdisciplinary, acutely aware of historical and cultural circumstance, sensitive to the insights of art and the creative life, and, most importantly, attentive to the presentation of soul in the multiple ways of human knowing.

However, beyond even the research model, is the unique approach to research, that Dr. Romanyshyn calls Alchemical Hermeneutics, which brings the unconscious into play. While all of his work, from the classroom to the clinic, is marked by a keen attention to image and dream, Alchemical Hermeneutics is precisely designed to integrate the unconscious depth of the research process into its explicit enactment. As "research with soul in mind," this approach is attentive to the ways in which we are called to our research projects. There is a calling not only to the activity of research but also something that the soul is asking us witness, to testify to, in the specific research topic. The "unfinished business of the ancestors," as Dr. Romanyshyn likes to say, lays claim on us and we honor them in our research activities. Recognition and service to this inherent, soulful value of research distinguishes Alchemical Hermeneutics and informs all of the academic programs at Pacifica from counseling to clinical, from mythology to ecological studies.

In introducing this volume of essays written by esteemed colleagues in honor of the many distinguished achievements of Dr. Romanyshyn's life work, I want to close with Robert's own words, a plea for us as a people to hear the urgency of the call from the world and all of her creatures, landscapes, and things.

> The task [at hand is one] of nurturing the birth of a new collective dream of the soul at a time when visions of the apocalypse increasingly threaten not only humanity but also, and perhaps more tragically, the innocent species with whom we share this planet. It is a (practice) devoted to anamnesis, to the difficult but necessary work of un-forgetting, a work that requires journeys of return, re-collection and re-membrance. Individually and collectively we are awakening to our condition of being orphans in exile and to the vocation to begin the journey of homecoming. The gesture of the soul in these moments of awakening is the backward glance and its mood is one of reverie. The backward glance is the occasion when the marginalized, forgotten and ignored aspects of our collective, cultural, and individual lives are re-gathered for the sake of an-other beginning. It is the moment of letting go of unexamined ways of knowing and being, and the occasion when one's heritage might be taken up as a destiny and one's destiny as a vocation. It is the Orphic moment of the soul, which opens one to the aesthetic truths of the heart, to those reasons of

the heart that reason does not know. My hope is that [my work] provides an occasion for these moments and an oasis for fellow travelers in service to freeing the energies of the soul for this journey.

In honor of Dr. Robert D. Romanyshyn and all he has offered to the academy, to Pacifica Graduate Institute, and to those we hold dear, I am pleased to introduce this volume of essays and reflections.

Editor's Introduction
Michael P. Sipiora

"You know that I am just about the only one around here who is going to talk to you about those things." It was in the first week of the Fall semester of 1978 and I was at the University of Dallas to study psychology. We had just had a class in which I had posed existential questions about psychological life. I was sitting in the hall outside the classroom and it was my professor who spoke. This was the beginning of a thirty-five year conversation with Robert D. Romanyshyn.

Among the things I most appreciate about Romanyshyn is how well he thinks and writes. Whether it is "Bob" the phenomenologist, "Robert" the Jungian, or that distinctive mix that makes up his version of Imaginal psychology, Romanyshyn is always worth reading. So, I thought what better way to celebrate his 70th birthday than that for a group of his friends and colleagues to write essays for a Festschrift. Indeed, all the contributors to the Festschrift have this in common: we have been in wonderful conversation with Robert…passionate, provocative, profound conversations about a wide range of matters relevant to the soul.

I invited the contributors to write a scholarly essay about whatever they wished, whatever drew their passion. While it may or may not relate to Romanyshyn's work, I asked that they compose an essay that they would like him to read. As if in self-portrait, Romanyshyn often refers to the figures of the philosopher, the psychologist, and the poet. Accordingly, I have grouped the essays in this volume as Philosophical, Psychological, and Poetic Reflections. The placement of essays under one rather than another of these headings has been somewhat arbitrary. Not surprisingly, most—if not all—of the contributions could have been included under more than one heading. I take this to reflect the radically interdisciplinary character of Romanyshyn's thought which each of the contributors celebrate in their essays.

A special note of thanks goes to Chancellor Stephen Aizenstat for his introduction to and enthusiastic support for this volume, and also gratitude to Pacifica Graduate Institute for funding its publication.

I am privileged to offer this Festschrift to Robert on the festive occasion of his 70th birthday with the esteem and warm wishes of the contributors. As the Polish saying goes, *Sto Lat:* "Good luck, good cheer, may you live a hundred years!"

Philosophical Reflections

'Bringing Heidegger Home': Finding Myself Thrown — and Picking Myself Back Up Again[1]

Scott D. Churchill

Preface

I present this paper in honor of Robert Romanyshyn — my dear friend, long-time colleague, and fellow traveler in life's journey – with whom I share a deep and abiding love for the thought of Martin Heidegger. My long personal history with Robert goes back to the day that he interviewed me at the Pittsburgh Zoo for a teaching position at the University of Dallas. While pondering the lived-worlds and eating habits of gorillas and chimpanzees, our discussions often circled back to phenomenology – and in particular, to Heidegger. For my contribution to this Festschrift, I have prepared this excerpt from the paper I presented in Montreal at the 31st Annual Meeting of the International Human Science Research Conference. Robert was sitting right in my line of vision, and the look on his face as I read my paper was something that I'll never forget: He kept looking up from our moments of eye contact, as though pausing to reflect analytically on what I was revealing about myself. It is this deeply felt connection between us that I wish to honor by presenting here in abbreviated form my Heideggerian reflections on trauma and recovery.

Introduction

> To be ill, even with just a trivial illness, as much as with a mortal illness, means, above all, to experience things in a different way, to be different yonder, to live in another, maybe hardly different, maybe completely different, world. Jan van den Berg (1972, p. 45)

What I would like to do in this paper is to demonstrate how a Heideggerian sensitivity to the meanings latent in our own challenges of living can serve to orient us, especially in times of difficulty, toward finding our path, and indeed, our foothold on the paths that we have chosen.

In his important essay *Phenomenological Interpretations of Aristotle*,

---

1 This is a condensed version of Heideggerian Pathways Through and Recovery. *The Humanistic Psychologist*, 41(3).

Heidegger (1922/1989) observed:

> The basic problem of philosophy has to do with the being of factical life in the [peculiar] how [*jeweiligen Wie*] of its being-addressed and being-interpreted at particular times … (pp. 246-247)

The transcript of Heidegger's subsequent lecture course in the summer of 1923 begins with this statement:

> *Facticity* is the designation we will use for the character of the being of "our" "own" Dasein. More precisely, this expression means: *in each case* "this" Dasein in its being-there *for a while at the particular time…* (p 5)

Further on, he wrote:

> Hermeneutics has the task of making the Dasein which is in each case our own *accessible to this Dasein itself* with regard to the character of its being, communicating Dasein to itself in this regard, *hunting down the alienation from itself with which it is smitten* (emphasis added) … In hermeneutics what is developed for Dasein is a possibility of its becoming and being for itself in the manner of an *understanding* of itself. (p 11)

The hermeneutics (or self-interpretation) belonging to my own psychological life will be the focus of my reflection here, as I refer back to the particular time of my recovery from traumatic injury.

I. The Hermeneutic Situation

Following a car accident in February of 2011, I spent three months suffering with discomfort in my right shoulder, undergoing several rounds of physical therapy and eventually an MRI that revealed only one of what turned out to be four ruptured rotator cuff tendons. Thinking that this would be a 'simple' repair, I was allowed to attend my conferences in Oxford and Washington and then return for surgery. Given that I had been planning a 15-month sabbatical since the previous fall, it is an understatement to say that the sudden realization that I needed surgery – followed by several months of intensive physical rehabilitation – came as a profound disturbance to my anticipated trajectory for the rest of the year. I had been 'living towards' this projected future, a sabbatical that would take me to far away places. Indeed, part of the way that I 'while' my time in my everyday life is to be anticipating my future travels: I imagine where I will be journeying, and the closer I get to the time of the departure, the more the 'center' of my existence seems to shift from my present 'here and now' to my future adventures.

Thus the diagnosis came as a shock, and required me to immediately begin rethinking my plans for the next year. Just four days after my return from giving my first Keynote, I would find myself lying in bed at midnight after outpatient surgery earlier in the afternoon -- with a 24-hour nerve block wearing off after just eight hours, enduring a night of interminable agony. For the next eight weeks my life was confined to shuffling back and forth between the resting place in my bedroom and a couch in my living room. During this stretch of time in which daily routine became monotonous and unfulfilling, I found myself trying to put myself back onto some timeline. It seemed as though I should be able to, at the end of my recovery, just wind the clock back to where I 'would have' been.

The odd thing was that I discovered the further I plodded along in my recovery, the less I was able to see my way back to June 30th, which would have been the 'experiential' start of my sabbatical. Indeed, as my own sense of temporality became relegated to the subjunctive – to what "would have been" – I realized more and more how really lost I was in the 'here and now'. My present had always been lived as a 'being oriented towards the future' -- and now it had become a limbo from which I was seeking refuge in the "might have been." The Heraclitian 'river of time' was still flowing; only, by now I had drifted far downstream – and all I could do was try to look back and find that dock from which my ship was supposed to have sailed so many months earlier. How could I swim against the flow to get back there? I finally realized that I was fighting the flow of time itself, in a refusal to acknowledge 'this' present – this *being-in-limbo*– as my true state of affairs (my facticity).

It was during this struggle to reorient myself in time that Heidegger came to me. His notion of "thrown projection" kept occurring to me, in my spontaneous moments of 'taking stock'. Without a computer at home, my communications had become limited to what I could press out with my two thumbs on my cell phone – and even a sentence was enough to send searing pain into my shoulder. Still, during this time there was a strong impulse to be in contact, to seek support, to enter into dialogue, to try to find my bearings once more. And it was this notion of 'projecting ourselves forward from where we find ourselves situated' – and not from where we had stood several months ago – that kept coming to me. In this long stretch of time – this long, empty "while" of recovery – I realized that I needed to let go of my attachment to my sabbatical plan – an attachment that was holding me back from genuinely reorienting myself in the current moment.

At that point of letting go, I began to imagine my way forward again – this time, from where I found myself situated now, in this new present that had become the life that I was living. Just as Sartre (1943/1956) had rejected Hegel's notion that one's essence is to be found in 'what has been', so I had learned to reject the idea that my essence could any longer be found in 'what might have been'. It was Heidegger who had reoriented our understanding of our essence to be something we can only find in our future, in our "to be." And that 'to be' is something that is inextricably bound to our facticity – to where we *find ourselves situated.* Whether we like it or not, we have to *go through* – rather than circling back around – the circumstances that befall us. And this *going through* involves a *centering* of ourselves in our recoveries, our rehabilitations, even our relapses – rather than seeing these as obstacles or impediments.

Learning to center ourselves in 'where we find ourselves situated' – in what Heidegger called *Befindlichkeit* -- is the first step towards 'authenticity', or finding *one's own* way into the future.

II. Reflection upon Factical Life

Talk (*Logos*), Heidegger tells us in his lecture course, is the "average manner in which Dasein takes itself in hand, holds onto itself, and preserves itself." (1923/1999, p 25). "This talk [and we would extend this to the written word in the form of diaries or even text messages] is thus the how in which a definite manner of Dasein's *having-been-[already]-interpreted* stands at its disposal" (p. 25). And thus my looking back upon text messages sent in the middle of the night during my convalescence has become *a mode of access* to my own experience. At one point, reflecting back upon my experience of recovery, I wrote this down:

> In the depths of the pain and despair, I can register only the loss of
> what I had possessed before: possibility, travel plans, self-realization

as a scholar, self-fulfillment as an individual… I cannot let go of all the plans I had made for my full-year sabbatical; I cannot let go of the idea that I've been pulled off-course; that where I find myself, is not where I am supposed to be.

I keep wishing to get back on track. It is just like when I was hit by a car as a fifth grader on my way to the bus stop. After flying in the air and landing on the pavement, I got myself up, collected my torn briefcase that had broken the headlight of the big Chevy that hit me, and positioned myself into the line with the other children waiting for the bus. And then I lost consciousness and fell to the ground. In both traumas, there is this desire to put myself back where I belong — standing inline for the bus, on my way to school; or, putting myself back at the start of my sabbatical, about to leave everything behind and set off for far away places.…

Could it be that I "remembered" Heidegger's "existentials" of thrownness, projection, and 'thrown projection' — at precisely the moment that I was discovering for myself how I needed to proceed with my life? And was this 'remembering' itself the 'hermeneutics' belonging to my own facticity? Did my own self-interpretation here take the form of remembering Heidegger?

Heidegger's (1923/1999) "hermeneutics of facticity" leads us directly to "a look at everydayness" (page 65). This looking [*schauen*] is a "looking at" [*an-schauen*, or "intuition"] that consists of "bringing a concrete situation phenomenally into view in accord with the stretches of the awhileness of its temporal particularity and having a look at how, in this awhileness -- as the how of the everydayness which is closest to us -- the world is being encountered" (page 65). So how was I "whiling" my time during my recovery?

It is interesting, looking back on my diary, that I would do something striking whenever I found myself awake in the middle of the night: I would reach over with my good arm, and turn on the light! Somehow, the darkness felt more alienating — especially when darkness is meant for sleeping, which I couldn't do either because of the pain or the pain medicine. And when I couldn't sleep, it seemed an insult to my consciousness to be surrounded by just darkness. Turning on the light re-established the possibility of my 'being-alongside' things encountered in the world: it re-established my interest in reading the books that I kept next to my pillow; it opened the possibility of sending a message to someone who might be awake on the other side of the Atlantic. Heidegger's notion of 'de-severence' became a propos here: the cell phone became a means of deliverance from lonely solitude. Through it I was able to feel connected rather than abandoned.

It was in these late night privations and disruptions, that my *Jeweiligkeit* taught me what was most dear to me – it was in the *"long while"* of my solitary days (punctuated from time to time with generous visits from a number of friends) that I realized what was most important to me by its very absence: my *possibilities*. ... It was this "longwhile" of putting off my projects, delaying my sabbatical travels, that also brought to mind perhaps the purest sense of what Heidegger spent over a hundred pages talking about in his 1929-30 lecture course in Marburg: *Langweile.* The English translation "boredom" is an abstraction that does not do justice to the lived experience to which I am referring; *Langweile,* however, says it all – it was a 'long while' before I would start to recover. And the recovery itself from the *langweilig* post-surgical experience would teach me about what was fundamental to my life.

If the *essence* of each particular Dasein lies in the "way" in which we comport ourselves toward our Being (Heidegger, 1927/1962, p. 67), then moments of profound lostness in time -- *tiefe Langweile* or 'deeply long-while' -- reveal us to ourselves as fundamentally "thrown" and in search of a way of "projecting" ourselves "back into the throw" of our daily lives – even if only back into our *being-fallen*! In the 'long while' of recovery from any serious illness or injury, one finds little solace in the past, nor a satisfying anchorage in the present; not even Hegel's idea that the past is what truly defines us (*"das Wesen ist was gewesen ist"*) can comfort us in the long stretches of whiling our time away in isolation and 'long stretches of time' (or, in my case, isolated recovery from illness); for, our 'peculiar awhileness' here reveals the deeper truth of Heidegger's (1927/1972) radical reorientation of Hegel's backwards glance, when he wrote: *"Das 'Wesen' des Daseins liegt in seinem Zu-sein"* (Heidegger, 1927/1962, p. 42). Thus, instead of lying in the past, our essence lies in our *Existenz*, in our projection of ourselves into our "to-be", into our future [*Zukunft*]. It is in the 'not yet' rather than in what has 'already been' that we shall truly find ourselves.

At first, I could register only the loss of where I had stood positioned prior to my injury; but then I recalled that we as human beings are 'thrown projects' (or 'situated freedoms') and that whatever we do, it can only be from where we already stand. I would thus have to find new footing from where I was standing after my injury – and realized that letting go of my earlier 'projection of possibilities' would be the first step to 'recovery.' There was kind of a dialectic going on between my experience of recovery and my reflective understanding of what was happening to me -- until my life began to adapt and accommodate to my new situation, at which point I made peace with where I found myself, and from there was able to chart a new path for myself.

Looking beyond my own experience of recovery towards the possibility of a "general structure" of what might be called 'the recovery one's own Being', I am struck by the profound "thrownness" that defines all situations of illness and trauma: there is a way in which we cannot get beyond the particularity – the *Jemeinigkeit* – of each story of illness and trauma.

Conclusion

Part of the *Gelassenheit* of Heideggerian temporality is that the authentic Present builds and creates itself as the Past withdraws. Life continues from where we stand now: not from where we stood before. The main obstacle for my psychological recovery had been letting go of the "projects" or projections of myself from the situation I had for myself before everything changed. When changes occur in our present, so do all of our future projects -- and that can be as disturbing as the unwanted changes themselves! Part of what we have to do, is to find a way to incorporate into our new 'Situation' something to replace those very projects we had standing before us, before our setback. And then that former 'present' can slip gracefully into the 'past' -- As a new set of projects – of *to-be's* -- renews our sense of an anchorage in the future.

References

Heidegger, M. (1962). *Being and time* (J. MacQuarrie & E. Robinson, Trans.). New York: Harper & Row. (Original work published 1927)

Heidegger, M. (1972). *Sein und Zeit* (12th ed.). Tuebingen: Max Niemeyer Verlag. (Original edition published 1927)

Heidegger. M. (1989). Phaenomenologische Interpretationen zu Aristoteles (Anziege der hermeneutischen Situation). [Phenomenological interpretations of Aristotle (Indication of the hermeneutical situation).] *Dilthey Jahrbuch fuer Philosophie und Geschichte der Geisteswissenshaften 6, 237-274.* (Original essay composed in October 1922 and published 1989)

Heidegger, M. (1999). *Ontology -- The hermeneutics of facticity* (J. van Buren, Trans.). Bloomington: Indiana University Press. (Original lecture course presented 1923 and published 1988)

Heidegger, M. (2001). *Phenomenological interpretations of Aristotle: Initiation into phenomenological research* (R. Rojcewicz, Trans.). Bloomington: Indiana University Press. (Original lecture course presented 1921-1922 and published 1985)

Sartre, J.-P. (1956). *Being and nothingness: An essay in phenomenological ontology (H.* Barnes, Trans.). New York: Philosophical Library. (Original work published 1943)

van den Berg, J. H. (1972). *A different existence: Principles of phenomenological psychopathology.* Pittsburgh: Duquesne University Press.

The Heart of Buddhist Mythos:
Cultivating the Ethics of Compassion in an Interdependent World

Patrick Mahaffey

> A human being is part of the whole, called by us "Universe," a part limited in time and space. He experiences himself, his thoughts and feelings, as something separated from the rest—a kind of optical delusion of his consciousness. This delusion is a kind of prison for us, restricting us to our personal desires and to affection for a few persons nearest to us. Our task must be to free ourselves from this prison by widening our circle of compassion to embrace all living creatures and the whole of nature in its beauty.
>
> —Albert Einstein

Buddhism posits a profoundly moral perspective on life. The intricacies of Buddhist thought fascinate me, but what I find most compelling is the ethical aspect of the worldview. As an engaged scholar, I actively practice the traditions I research and teach. After years of Jungian analysis, I continue to work with shadow material, dreams, and active imagination. This depth psychological process is of great value, but contemplative practices from Hindu and Buddhist traditions are the core of my inner work. Meditation and self-inquiry, for example, have proven to be powerful methods for calming afflicting emotions, stabilizing the mind, and awakening the heart. Most importantly, these practices support the aspiration to cultivate a nonviolent way of life. Attempting to live in this way requires a conscious effort to move from preoccupation with one's personal well-being to a more inclusive concern for the welfare of others and the earth we inhabit. Negotiating the shift from an egocentric and ethnocentric stance to a more cosmocentric perspective is among the most critical challenges we face in the twenty-first century.

A *mythos* is a worldview that conveys an interrelated set of beliefs, attitudes, and values. The classical philosophical systems in Indian philosophy are known as *darshanas*. The word *darshana* derives from the verbal root *drish*, which means "to see," and thus is a way of seeing reality.

A *darshana* also embodies practices and a way of being in the world. The Buddha articulated a worldview that has been deeply influential in many Asian cultures and, more recently, in the West. This essay reflects upon selected teachings and practices that express the heart of the Buddhist vision of reality. Attention is given to the Buddha's assessment of the human condition, the purpose of Buddhist meditative practices, and how the wisdom of emptiness provides a basis for an ethics of compassion.

Four Noble Truths

Siddhartha Gotama, Prince of the Shakyas, awakened to Buddhahood more than twenty-five hundred years ago. As a historical figure, he lived during the fifth and sixth centuries B.C.E. in a small kingdom near what is now the border of Nepal and India (Chödzin 2000; Nakamura 2000, 2005). At the age of thirty-five he had a profound spiritual awakening in which he realized his true nature and the interdependent nature of reality. On a psychological level, we can view the Buddha as a fundamental archetype of humanity, an expression of the fully awakened mind, exemplifying the potential for enlightenment contained within all human beings (Goldstein, 1999, p. 9). His journey to awakening entailed the discovery of a path between sensory indulgence and asceticism. In other words, he grappled with opposites before discerning a path to wholeness that overcomes the sorrows that typify egocentric existence. After his awakening, in the Deer Park near Sarnath, he gave his first discourse on the teachings of the Middle Way that would subsequently be known as *buddhadharma*, the teachings of the Buddha.

The core of the Buddha's first discourse is the Four Noble Truths: suffering (*duhkha*), the origin of suffering (*samudaya*), the cessation of suffering (*nirodha*), and the eightfold path (*marga*) that leads to the cessation of suffering. The first of these is a sobering list of inconvenient truths: "Birth is suffering; aging is suffering; sickness is suffering; death is suffering; association with the unpleasant is suffering; dissociation from the pleasant is suffering; not to get what one wants is suffering" (Rahula, 1999, p. 66). In addition to physical pain, *duhkha* refers to emotional and psychological distress like grief, sorrow, lamentation, and despair. Beyond these affective states, there is a more subtle kind of suffering. Existential or psychological suffering entails the frustration, disappointment, and disillusionment we feel when life fails to live up to our expectations and when things do not go as we wish (Keown, 1996, pp. 46-47). Indeed, existence is unsatisfactory in one respect or another.

The second noble truth enunciated by the Buddha concerns the origin of this malaise. Traditional representations of the Buddha's teachings specify the cause as craving, desire, or attachment. In Pali the word for craving is *tanha* (Sanskrit: *trishna*), which literally means "thirst." Does the Buddha's second noble truth suggest that all desire is problematic? Many Buddhists contend that this would be a misunderstanding of the teaching. The word *tanha* has a more restricted meaning and connotes desire that is wrongly directed or excessive, as in addictive behavior or greed. While *tanha* is the crucial term in the Theravada system, the scholars of this tradition acknowledge that it is not the only cause of suffering but "the most palpable and immediate cause" (Tashi Tserling, 2005, p. 60). According to the Mahayana tradition, the root sources of suffering are said to be our fundamental ignorance of the true nature of existence and our afflictive emotions. Anger, arrogance, and wrong views are also said to be causes of suffering (p. 60; Nhat Hanh, 1998, pp. 21-22). Wholesome desires also exist and include the positive goals one has for oneself and others, such as the aspiration to attain nirvana and the wish that others be happy and free.

The first two noble truths provide a diagnosis of the human condition that many deem pessimistic. Yet, the third noble truth inspires. It boldly asserts that the cessation of suffering is possible: that we can give up our craving and reactivity and attain nirvana. Nirvana literally means "quenching" or "blowing out" and what is extinguished is the triple fire of craving, hatred, and ignorance. Nirvana is often misunderstood to be a nihilistic idea—a negation of existence—but it refers to the cessation of suffering rather than the literal annihilation of the person. As Keown (1996) observed, "It is clear that nirvana-in-this-life is a psychological and ethical reality, a transformed state of personality characterized by peace, deep spiritual joy, compassion, and a refined and subtle awareness" (p. 53). The fourth noble truth explains how the transition from suffering to nirvana is made and describes an eightfold path divided into three categories of ethical conduct (*shila*), meditation (*samadhi*), and wisdom (*prajna*). A practitioner trains in each of these three areas. Ethics includes right speech, right action, and right livelihood; meditation involves right effort, right mindfulness, and right concentration; and wisdom consists of right view and right thought. The eight elements of the path are not stages one passes through on the way to nirvana, but exemplify the ways in which ethics, meditation, and wisdom are to be cultivated on a continuing basis (p. 55).

Ethics and Meditation

Buddhist practice can be pictured as a three-tiered pyramid with wisdom at the apex. The second tier, which facilitates wisdom and makes it effective, is meditation practice. The first tier at ground level is ethical discipline (Wallace, 1999, p. 16). The basis for Buddhist ethics is grounded in our basic sameness as human beings. No matter what our situation, we all desire to be happy and to avoid suffering. As His Holiness the Dalai Lama has observed:

> My own view, which does not rely solely on religious faith or even on an original idea, but rather on common sense, is that establishing binding ethical principles is possible when we take as our starting point the observation that we all desire happiness and wish to avoid suffering. We have no means of discriminating between right and wrong if we do not take into account others' feelings, others' suffering. (Gyatso, 1999a, p. 28)

The implication of this relational perspective is clear: ethical conduct is not something that can be enforced from the outside but must grow out of a subjective understanding of what helps and what harms others, and it depends on whether others' feelings and rights have been considered. Ethics, therefore, must be grounded in compassion. At the same time, ethics flounders without mindfulness and the sense of the interconnectedness of all beings (Tashi Tserling, 2005, p. 126). This is where meditation and wisdom come into play.

All schools of Buddhism see meditation as the royal road to enlightenment. The general term for meditation in Buddhism is *bhavana*, which means "cultivation" or literally "making become." Meditation is the principal Buddhist strategy for making oneself what one wishes to be (Keown, 1996, p. 84). There are several types of Buddhist meditation and each serves a different, though complementary, purpose. The Buddha trained in the concentrative forms of meditation that led to lucid states of rapt absorption known as *samadhi*, a condition of complete and unwavering inner stillness. Yet, he left his meditation teachers because he came to see that entering into a state of trance, however blissful and serene, was temporary and thus not a permanent solution to suffering. Meditative states, like all others, are impermanent. These states fail to provide the philosophical insight into the nature of things that is needed for complete liberation. The

Buddha developed a new form of meditation called "insight meditation" or *vipashyana* (Pali: *vipassana*) to supplement the practices he learned from his teachers. In Buddhism, the traditional methods of meditation are referred to as "calming meditation" or *shamatha*. Generally, the two techniques of calming and insight are practiced back-to-back within the same session. Calming is used first to concentrate the mind, followed by insight to probe and analyze its contents (pp. 93-94). The goal of Buddhist practice is the attainment of *bodhichitta*, literally "the mind of enlightenment," which is often translated as "awakened heart" or "the altruistic mind." Bodhichitta refers to a deep longing to wake up from ignorance and delusion in order to help others do the same (Chödrön, 2006, p. 72).

Insight meditation is often described as analytical meditation. The analytical mind is used to penetrate the nature of things. Buddhists also engage in another type of meditation, the "heart practices" of loving-kindness, compassion, empathetic joy, and equanimity. These are called the "measureless states" because they may be expanded limitlessly (Wallace 1999). Loving-kindness practice involves cultivating an attitude of benevolence, friendship, and goodwill towards all living creatures. The meditator begins with herself as the object of goodwill, and then gradually extends the circle of benevolence to include her family, neighborhood, town, nation and, eventually, all persons without exception. Cultivating such universal good will frees the mind from partiality and prejudice. The other measureless states are cultivated in a similar way. By generating and expanding compassion in one's heart, the meditator identifies with the suffering of others, and through sympathetic joy rejoices in their happiness and good fortune. Cultivation of equanimity helps ensure that these dispositions are balanced and appropriate to the circumstance.

The Wisdom of Emptiness

The Theravada tradition focuses on the liberation of the individual practitioner. Around the beginning of the Common Era, a new emphasis emerged in the Mahayana ("Great Vehicle") tradition. The highest ideal in the Mahayana is a life dedicated to the well being of the world. Rather than seeking one's own liberation, the Mahayana places great emphasis on working to free others from suffering. This aim is exemplified in the ideal of the *bodhisattva*, a practitioner who vows to work tirelessly over countless lifetimes to lead others to nirvana. The shift is from self-interest to a more compassionate and inclusive concern for others, and it is grounded in the Mahayana teachings about emptiness.

"Emptiness" *(shunyata)* pertains to the principle of dependent origination *(pratitya samutpada)*, the notion "that all conditioned things and events in the universe come into being only as a result of the interaction of various causes and conditions" (Gyatso, 1997, p. 12). Nothing has independent or intrinsic identity of its own. When we realize that everything we perceive and experience arises in this way, our worldview changes. What appears as some kind of autonomous, objective reality does not fit with how things actually are. Once we understand the fundamental disparity between appearance and reality, we gain insight into the way our emotions work and how we react to events and objects. In the epigraph for this essay, Albert Einstein observed that human beings experience themselves as separate from the universe, a kind of "optical delusion of consciousness" that is a kind of prison for us. The Buddhist teaching on emptiness is the remedy for this misapprehension of reality. To understand emptiness is to appreciate our interdependency with all beings. Thich Nhat Hanh (1988) has coined a new term, "interbeing," to describe the reality of our fundamental interconnectedness (pp. 3-4). Emptiness, he observes, "means empty of a separate self. It is full of everything else, full of life" (p. 16).

Cultivating a Compassionate Heart

His Holiness the Dalai Lama teaches the Four Noble Truths in relation to two principles: the interdependent nature of reality and nonviolence. The first of these is the basis for all Buddhist philosophy. The second is the action taken by a Buddhist practitioner who has the view of the interdependent nature of reality. Nonviolence, he explains, "essentially means that we should do our best to help others and, if this is not possible, should at the very least refrain from hurting others" (Gyatso, 1997, p. 7). In his view, global crises are the result of long-standing negligence. The problems have their causes and conditions, and most of them arise when human emotions are out of control. If we want a happier humanity and a more peaceful world, we need to tackle the root of the problem. Although economic and political issues are genuine causes of suffering, the ultimate cause lies within the human heart. The Dalai Lama (1999b) insists that spiritual development means developing a good and compassionate heart (Gyatso, p. 61). Rigid hearts give rise to fundamentalist beliefs that, in turn, lead to conflict and war (Chödrön, 2006, pp. 21-22). From a Buddhist point of view, our task is to replace hatred with love and compassion and to bring about change through nonviolence and nonaggression. This is a radical stance in a world characterized by terrorism and fear. Buddhists take a long-term perspective on these matters. The nature of mind is such that if certain mental qualities are developed on a sound basis, they will always remain and can even increase (Gyatso, 2000, p. 33). Sadly, the reverse is also true. As Shantideva observed, "If these long-lived, ancient, aggressive patterns of mind that are the wellspring not only of unceasing woe, that lead to my own suffering and the suffering of others, if these patterns still find their lodging safe within my heart, how can joy and peace in this world ever be found?" (as cited in Chödrön, 2006, p. 27).

The Buddhist worldview is an ancient tradition that transmits ethical principles and values that are deeply needed in the twenty-first century; it is a perspective that complements and potentially deepens the depth psychology of the West. More importantly, Buddhist tradition provides us with practices that enable us to embody these principles and values in our lives. Put another way, the heart of Buddhist mythos—the teachings and practices that cultivate compassion—provide us with the means by which we may become psychologically and ethically responsible individuals. The challenge is clear: like Siddhartha, we are called to awaken from our ignorance about the deepest sources of human suffering. We are also enjoined to make the journey from egocentric complacency to compassionate concern for others in a profoundly interconnected world. The process begins by genuinely acknowledging the myriad forms of suffering that appear before us; it then generates insight or wisdom as we inquire deeply into the causes and conditions that perpetuate suffering. If we are sincere in this effort, we must be willing to change the way we see and the way we live. When we take our meditation seat, we must face our particular forms of self-deception and replace the hatred and aggression in our hearts with love and compassion. The journey is a voyage into the core of our humanity that requires a willingness to expand our circle of compassion to acknowledge all sentient beings as worthy of the happiness for which we ourselves long.

References

Chödrön, P. (2006). *Practicing peace in times of war*. Boston, MA: Shambhala.
Chödzin Kohn, S. (2000). *The awakened one: A life of the Buddha*. Boston, MA: Shambhala.
Goldstein, J. (1999). The Buddha's sacred journey. In S. Salzberg (Ed.), *Voices of insight* (pp.

9-21). Boston, MA: Shambhala.

Gyatso, T., the Fourteenth Dalai Lama. (1997). *The four noble truths* (T. Jinpa, Trans. & D. Side, Ed.). London, England: Thorsons, 1997.

Gyatso, T., the Fourteenth Dalai Lama. (1999a). *Ethics for a new millennium.* New York, NY: Riverdale Books.

Gyatso, T., the Fourteenth Dalai Lama. (1999b). *Live in a better way: Reflections on truth, love and happiness* (R. Singh. Ed.). New York, NY: Viking Compass.

Gyatso, T., the Fourteenth Dalai Lama. (2000). *The meaning of life: Buddhist perspectives on cause and effect* (J. Hopkins, Trans. & Ed.). Boston, MA: Wisdom.

Keown, D. (1996). *Buddhism: A very short introduction.* Oxford, England: Oxford University Press.

Nakamura, H. (2000). *Gotama Buddha: A biography based on the most reliable texts, volume one* (G. Sekimori, Trans.). Tokyo, Japan: Kosei.

Nakamura, H. (2005). *Gotama Buddha: A biography based on the most reliable texts, volume two* (G. Sekimori, Trans.). Tokyo, Japan: Kosei.

Nhat Hanh, T. (1998). *The heart of the Buddha's teaching: Transforming suffering into peace, joy, and liberation: The four noble truths, the noble eightfold Path, and other basic Buddhist teachings.* Berkeley, CA: Parallax Press.

Nhat Hanh, T. (1988). *The heart of understanding: Commentaries on the Prajnaparamita Heart Sutra.* Berkeley, CA: Parallax Press.

Rahula, W. (Trans.). (1999). The first sermon of the Buddha. In J. Smith (Ed.), *Radiant mind: Essential Buddhist teachings and texts* (pp. 65-66). New York, NY: Riverhead Books.

Tashi Tserling, Geshe. (2005). *The four noble truths.* (G. Mcdougall, Ed.). Somerville, MA: Wisdom.

Wallace, B. Alan. (1999). *Boundless heart: The cultivation of the four immeasurables* (Z. Houshmand, Ed.). Ithaca, NY: Snow Lion.

Mother & History: A Tribute to Romanyshyn and Merleau-Ponty

Kareen Malone

> If I had a boat
> I'd go out on the ocean
> And if I had a pony
> I'd ride him on my boat
> And we could all together
> Go out on the ocean
> Me upon my pony on my boat
> - Lyle Lovett

This is not an essay of documentation where academic authority serves as the roots of legitimation and founding of the community of ideas (Longino, 1990). Despite all efforts at (authoritarian or democratic) clarity, ideas are thankfully mis-understood all of the time (Feyerabend, 1987; Zizek's critique of Habermas, Zizek, 1989). This essay about Robert Romanyshyn does not even pursue a noble university discourse that stumbles upon epistemic breaks, honors its own accidents, is restrained by careful argument, or is justified by cautious research. I fear for the future of this university nobility, even with all of its flaws. When I said I needed to work on a review on Lacan and could not do "enrollment management" on a web-based system over the weekend, a staff member genuinely offered help. She said, "I'll train you in the enrollment system if you will train me in Lacan." Splitting the difference was irrelevant. But that is another post-Fordist conundrum.

Why then should the following deviate from its obvious precariously noble academic context? Robert Romanyshyn is a university professor and so am I. One would thus think that a University discourse, buttressed by citations and streaming lines of argument would be an appropriate form of engagement. Yet Romanyshyn does not really "do" university discourse in its true, naïve, but often incisive form; yes he reads books, looks at pictures, and writes words. He remains a proper thief. But, he leaves one fundamental aspect of university discourse neglected: university discourse tries to replace loss with knowledge (Lacan, 1991). Instead Romanyshyn incorporates what that question of loss means, its pulsation in time. To use Freud's framework (1921), there where the representative of the representation has been inscribed and then erased, there where in a moment a subject has been marked as different (Lacan, 1970), university discourse fails. It fails because it performs a further erasure or because it is based in making a whole, a uni-verse. While fantasy madly splices an image to an articulation to render a sustained relation to loss, conscious knowledge, particularly university knowledge, renders the captivating *extimacy/intimacy* of the image subordinate to exchangeable pieces of knowledge (Miller, 1994).

Romanyshyn, like Merleau-Ponty, like Lacan, wants to attempt to orient his narrative to the body-world relationship as a relation to the lost object. The latter two authors approach the topic a tad differently, and Romanyshyn bears a closer affinity to Merleau-Ponty in his ontological "referent." Romanyshyn, tempered by Heidegger, may be a sort of go-between, knowing that history is knotted with psyche; that Einstein and Picasso encounter the same impasses within their historical moment (Romanyshyn, 1989).

Merleau-Ponty answers more to the terms of philosophy, e.g. materialism, logical positivism, and idealism as defined by philosophical debate (Merleau-Ponty, 2012), while Lacan has to address the suffering person to whom he listens. He has to time an intervention which is not anchored in a knowledge of the world. The following quotation shows the difference. It is a response by Merleau-Ponty to Lacan's work via Freud and represents a certain investment in the everyday prosaic body versus the narrative of the client, discontinuous and about something that tears himself from himself:

> Now I will perhaps not say, as does Dr. Lacan, that everything is clear in Freud....I will confess that the Signorelli story, to which you have again alluded, always irritates me. When one reads this text, as many other psychoanalytic texts, and one is not initiated in psychoanalysis, either through practice or experience, one is always struck by the fact that Freud wishes to turn things around and not take them as they appear. (Phillips, 1996, p. 83)

Yet, even for a philosopher, there is something of a clinician in Merleau-Ponty's work and of a thinker who rests at a particular interstice. Conversely, being a clinician does not guarantee that you are not a university professor in clinical drag. The distinguishing characteristic of an impoverished psychoanalysis or clinical approach is the confusion of interpretation with a certain intellectual description of a client's current behavior towards the therapist, his intimate others, or a slip, parapraxis, or dream. This is why in part there is all that talk of relationship in psychoanalysis and psychotherapy as if it were something personal to compensate for the intellectualism that lays at the root of the practice, with its diagnoses, speculations, and normativity (Yalom, 2001). When one has already removed the point of one's personal sacrifice from the analytic act (Lacan, 2006), he or she has to add the intangible stakes back in, in the guise (semblance) of his or her "real" person. This is not the dimension in which the work is done. In contrast, Romanyshyn is rich rather than impoverished in drawing on the clinic; he shows appropriate clinical modesty in part because his "tools" are image and narrative as poesis, the *bien dire*, as Lacan would word it (Aguirre, 2011).

Merleau-Ponty, Lacan and Romanyshyn know that truth does not have the status of knowledge (Nobus, 2005; Lacan & Merleau-Ponty, Merleau-Ponty, 1964). Both thus begin by acknowledging the limit point of knowledge and attempting to articulate an ethical aesthetics in its stead. This understanding renders Romanyshyn's understanding of psychological life something particular – although I suppose a psychologist can study many things that we say and do. But there is a singularity here intertwined with a body born in history.

For Merleau-Ponty and Romanyshyn, there is a knowledge, a pre-reflective knowing before the doubling of self-reflection. This is a knowledge of depth as some in psychoanalysis would name it and distinguish it, as this latter formulation means unconscious knowledge, which is the acephalic knowledge of the drive, repetition, transference, fantasy stripped down (Lacan, 2003). In *Technology as Symptom and Dream*, Romanyshyn will speak of the earth's knowledge, the indecipherable calling of the maternal body, a recollection of a similar formulation from Merleau-Ponty (Phillips, 1996). This is captured in the idea of the *flesh* of the world as maternal body, and its insubstantial substrate, the body logic of the invisible that substantiates or realizes embodiment and evokes the gesture (Merleau-Ponty, 1964; Romanyshyn, 1989).

Herein lie the elements of a form of embodiment that Romanyshyn brings very close to a definitional formulation; loss, erased history, phantasm. Without seeing these elements as the structuration of dasein, we would read a nostalgia for a mother who *only misses* us. Instead she misses some other, that keeps us guessing, giving a genesis to a desire beyond in her gaze at us (Mieli, 2000). This "pre-reflective" knowledge worked to the bone by Romanyshyn, so tied to loss, to embodiment, to the unsayable that founds a world can be expressed, made real, humanized in many ways. As Freud talks about in *Group Psychology and the Analysis of the Ego*, it is a cultural necessity. In his Postscript to this essay, Freud relates this loss to a murder of the father, a murdered father that is replaced by a pact, a renunciation and a memory that spawns imagination, a loss that becomes the enigmatic desire of mother-making-a-world. This loss, this enigmatic desire that will never be realized founds in myth, religion, art, mysticism, physics; its immediate draw is found in fascination, horror, beauty, compulsion, and unrelenting desire (Romanyshyn, 1989; Lacan, 1990; Fanon, 1967). Romanyshyn, following a tradition that is both analytic and phenomenological, evokes reflections upon the image to tease out this pre-grounding that is often relegated to the divine, or, if we want to be both serious and radical about it, to the founding of the psyche. This is what Romanyshyn uses image for – he knows and stands by the ethics of a psychologist, by asking the originary question, asked by Freud, Lacan, Merleau-Ponty – what is psychological life?

Psychological life is a psychoanalytic matter (for me at least). Without Romanyshyn actually asking what it was, I am not sure I could have heard it in psychoanalysis. Romanyshyn is one of those thieves of psychoanalysis; there were a number in the twentieth century in psychoanalysis, for example, Horney, Abraham; some gravitated toward weak points in Freud; ideas still under development, like Kohut's interest in narcissism, Winnicott's invention of the transitional object (where Freud's story of the fort-da meets a pediatrician's examination of the primordial object). Others seemed to make a full theory of a piece from Freud (1986) and made it go a long way. Some may say that about Lacan and language. Others may say the same about the North American fascination with countertransference and transference. There are schools in which analysis of resistance through transference has pretty much replaced dream analysis, so selective Freud much like selective scripture in itself does not in itself assure that one has purloined the real jewel or merely given place to the obvious or ideological in a new lexicon. We get what makes sense, not what may be more urgent for the needed re-imagination of culture.

For Romanyshyn, what is needed is more tied to image, but its stakes are not about the rational subject of psychology or even the felt body, or any other piece of current social knowledge that cross-pollinates with the vortex of affects, narratives, and images that enter the clinic. Rather one is bringing forth a body inhabited by a subject who can live in the world. Referring to the painter in "Eye and Mind", Merleau-Ponty writes:

> The painter's vision is not a view upon the outside, a merely physical optical relation with the world. The World no longer stands before him through representation; rather, it is the painter to whom the things of the world give birth by a sort of concentration or coming into being of the visible. Ultimately the painting relates to nothing at all among experienced things unless it is first of all "autofigurative". It is a spectacle of something only by being a spectacle of nothing, by breaking the "skin of things"[1] to show how things become things, how the world becomes world. (Merleau-Ponty, 1964, p. 181)

The Romanyshyn that threw my work on a Lacanian course, was one that recognized that the later Heidegger and Merleau-Ponty grapple with a problem nestled within the logic of perception, *what you see is what you don't get*, contrary to the popular phrase. To be more precise, both were working the street of an ontological issue of the grounds of self-consciousness, the before, within embodiment. Although Heidegger seemed to veer toward the press of language, being the post-modern daddy that gets to be everyone's bête noir, Merleau-Ponty, moved from the gestalt of an action in the world, as founding an originary structure, to sublimation, i.e. to seeing a painting, to psychoanalysis, to the flesh of the world and towards the drive – although I am not sure one would place him there ultimately. For Merleau-Ponty, act and perception are still key, but the flesh of the world is found in the admixture of subject and object in what catches your eye. He separates eye and gaze, and realizes that we look at what looks back at us. Romanyshyn takes this insight into the heart of psychology, just as Lacan made much of this separation of eye and gaze and speaks in a significant way about Merleau-Ponty on this very point in his eleventh seminar in a chapter on the gaze – the gaze is an object of the drive – that which makes a body out of an event / encounter with the Other (Lacan, 1981). But it is that part of the Other which Lacan calls the real or the impossible, i.e. what is not articulable in the present tense of consciousness, but a noumena within materiality that dictates an aesthetic act or an epistemic break as in science; the implication of subjectivity, nay its beginnings are there. For Merleau-Ponty, the gaze draws our sight and beckons our gesture (Merleau-Ponty, 1964; Lacan, 1981). Romanyshyn is in this tradition as well, but appeals to language more essentially, as does Heidegger, through his reference to

---

[1] The Papin sisters were quoted as answering that they wanted to know the secret of life when asked about their murder of their two very respectable bourgeois mistresses whom they had served faithfully for years. The gaze of things is created as such by a mediation that allows an autofigurative painting (Clement, 1983). Merleau- Ponty refers to the seeing that "pre-writes" the seen.

metaphor and to the tensions within cultural history (Romanyshyn, 1982).

Romanyshyn's path is in part prepared, Lacan says, by the bringing forth of the limits of the visible, of perception, of vision as one's root metaphor, within philosophy itself, particularly any spin off of any all-knowing vision. But Lacan will take a different turn, one that attests to the fact of there being a psychological life that is essentially indebted to our speaking, to our culture, to our embodiment, but yet, as a matter of the *parle-être* (Milner, 1990). For him at least, when we become speaking, we are encircled in the form of address and subjected to three forms of the Other, the imaginary-same other or the other guy; the Symbolic Other, the cultural law of language and limit, and the other as the *object a*, what falls out, but resides (Pavon-Cuellar, 2010). The imaginary other interests a number of psychologists, but what is most interesting is what is uncanny within our counterpart. The Symbolic Other, filtered through the mother tongue, stacks representations, limits translation, makes metaphor a companion of being human forever, the *object a* is what is the dead stop of the image – the look that looks back, the tone of voice, the blank moment.

Despite the evocation of history and metaphor, Romanyshyn does not go in this linguistic direction, buying a certain view of language as representational rather than as a representative of a representation of a repressed encounter (Freud, 1921). He is suspicious of utilizing the structural effects of syntax and the debris of language, the calligraphy of the letter. Romanyshyn's awareness of loss will be captured in an essential aesthetics that can be within or beyond the beautiful and his awareness of the historic cuts that necessarily render the human. There is this tension in Romanyshyn's work between a nostalgia that pays the debt to an inevitable loss – a loss that for me binds the human to speaking and the image that is a fantasy in relation to that traumatic or tragic loss, and a yearning for a cosmology that might ease the suffering of that loss. For what is essentially missing has been honored in different ways (there is a loss that can always be "answered" by cosmology or the bill of rights (Fink, 2002; Parker et. al., 2000). In either case, there will be a gap in the answer. How the gap is played, by technology directing the drives, death being given to divine design, these responses of our being give body to a subject that is not without consequences, in its shifting efforts to be in relation to what is impossible to articulate.

Within this exact context, Lacan sees a limit to Merleau-Ponty that speaks to what Romanyshyn is working with in his reflections on culture and psychological life.

Let us say this because Merleau-Ponty does not seem to take this step....[h]is motive being that scientific construction should always come back to perception. On the contrary, everything shows that the Galilean dynamics annexed the heavens to the earth, at the heavy cost though, of introducing what we nowadays feel in the experience of the astronaut: a body that can open and close itself weighing nothing and bearing on nothing. (Lacan, 1982, p. 74)

Still one sees that perception is "really" an image, an in-mixing that is the subject as object, and sometimes, it is just a line, a mark of difference, a color, a spot, an object that is nothing in itself. This I think is a different sense of the literal than Romanyshyn's (1982) interrogation of the non-metaphoric within science, rather like the image, the literal is like pure sound – the littoral – a shifting mark, a cusp, to which the human is called close to what is most and least human. We are here at the point in the drawing that Georgia O'Keefe would call, with her penchant for too-close enormous flowers, slits in nothingness. The same intermingling, materially full yet empty structurally, is the perennial latency of phenomenology, is what Romanyshyn taps in the interrogation of the image; he taps that truly psychological dimension that is "between words", forbidden, and that must appear in style, in image, in a logic of the body that refers to the Other's gaze. Slavoj Zizek (Zizek, S., Santner, E.L., & Reinhard, K., 2005) suggests that in feudal times humans were placed / inscribed into the field subtended by the Other's gaze, but that field was protected or mediated by God's benevolent gaze, defining faith itself. In modernity, the subject defines herself as outside of the Other's gaze (internal experience), but in a sense we are simply less protected against that Other's gaze (see p. 178). As Romanyshyn notes, Warhol can want to be a machine, and *the what* that we are for the Other is contingent and sometimes terrifying. But there is a seeking for more or less room to breathe, more or less room for imagination, for desire, for forgiveness. This is the ethical key of Robert's work.

References

Aguirre, M.-C. (2011). Bulimia, anxiety, and the demand of the other. In: Y. G. Baldwin, K. Malone & T. Svolos (Eds.). (pp. 177 -186). *Lacan and Addiction*. London: Karnac Press.

Clement, C. (1983). *The lives and legends of Jacques Lacan*. New York: Colombia University

Press.

Cuéllar, D.P. (2010). *From the conscious interior to an exterior unconscious.* London: Karnac Press.

Fanon, F. (1967). *Black skin white masks.* New York: Grove Press. (Original work published 1952)

Feyerabend, P. (1987). *Farewell to reason.* New York: Verso.

Fink, B. (2002). Knowledge and science: Fantasies of the whole. In: J. Glynos and Y Stavrakakis. *Lacan and Science.* London: Karnac, pp. 167-178.

Freud, S. (1921). *Group psychology and the analysis of the ego.* In J. Strachey (Ed. & Trans.), *The standard edition of the complete psychological works of Sigmund Freud (Vol.18)* (pp. 67-143). London: Hogarth Press.

Freud, S. (1958). Recommendations to physicians practicing psychoanalysis. In J. Strachey (Ed. & Trans.) *The standard edition of the complete psychological works of Sigmund Freud (Vol.12)* (pp. 11-120) London: Hogarth Press. (Original work published 1912)

Freud, S. (1986). Observations on transference love (Further recommendations on the technique of psychoanalysis). In J. Strachey (Ed. & Trans) *The standard edition of the complete psychological works of Sigmund Freud (Vol.12)* (*p. 157)* London: Hogarth Press. (Original work published 1914)

Lacan, J. (1970). Of structure as an inmixing of an otherness prerequisite to any subject whatever. In R. Macksey & E. Donato (Eds.). *The structuralist controversy* (pp. 186-200). Johns Hopkins: Baltimore. (Lecture given in 1966)

Lacan, J. (1981). *The four fundamental concepts of psychoanalysis.* (J.-A. Miller, Ed. & A. Sheridan, Trans.). New York: Norton. (Original work published 1973)

Lacan, J. (1982). Merleau-Ponty: In Memoriam, *Review of Existential Psychology and Psychiatry*, 18, 73-82.

Lacan, J. (1991). *The seminar of Jacques Lacan: Book XVII: The other side of psychoanalysis,* (J.-A. Miller, Ed. R. Grigg, Trans.). New York: Norton. Original work published in 1991.

Lacan, J. (1990). Names of the Father. In *Television. (J. Copjec. Ed., D. Hollier, R. Kraus, & A. Michelson, Eds.). (pp. 81-96)., NY: Norton.* (Original work 1974)

Lacan, J. (2003). *The seminar of Jacques Lacan: The knowledge of the psychoanalyst,* (C. Gallagher, Trans.) London: Karnac Press.Lacan, J. (2006). Variations on the standard treatment. In B. Fink (Trans.), *Écrits.* New York: W.W. Norton & Company. (Original work published 1955)

Longino, H. (1990). *Science as social knowledge.* Princeton, NJ: Princeton University Press.

Merleau-Ponty, M. (1964). Eye and mind. In *The primacy of perception,* (J. Edie, Ed). (pp. 159-92). Chicago, Il.: Northwestern Press.

Merleau-Ponty, M. (2012). *The phenomenology of perception.* (D.A. Landes, Trans.) New York : Routledge. (Original work published in 1945)

Mieli, P. (2000). Femininity and the limits of theory. In *The subject of Lacan.* (Malone & Friedlander, Eds.). (pp. 265-278). Albany, NY: State University Press.

Miller, J. (1994). Extimité. In: M. Bracher, M. Alcorn, R. Corthell, and F. Massardier-Kenney, eds. *Lacanian theory and discourse.* New York: New York University Press, pp. 74-87.

Milner, J. C. (1990). *For the love of language.* (A. Banfield, Trans.) New York: St. Martin's Press.

Nobus, D. & Quinn, M. (2005). *Knowing nothing saying stupid: Elements for a psychoanalytic epistemology.* London: Routledge.

O'Keefe, G. (2010). From notes on the exhibit: Abstraction. Georgia O'Keefe Museum. Sante Fe, MN.

Parker, R. Barbosa R. , & Aggleton P. (Eds.) (2000). Framing the sexual subject: The politics of gender, sexuality, and power. Berkeley: University of California Press.

Phillips, J. (1993). Lacan and Merleau-Ponty: The configuration of Psychoanalysis and Phenomenology. In *Disseminating Lacan.* (D. Pettigrew & F. Raffoul, Eds.) Albany, New York: State University of New York Press.

Romanyshyn, R.(1982). *Psychological life: From science to metaphor.* Austin: University of Texas Press.

Romanyshyn, R. (1989). *Technology as symptom and dream.* London / New York: Routledge.

Yalom, I. (2001). *The gift of therapy.* New York: Harper Collins

Žižek, S. (1989). *The sublime object of ideology.* London: Verso.

Žižek, S. (1997) Multiculturalism, or the cultural logic of multinational capitalism. *New Left Review, 225,* 28-51.

Žižek, S., Santner, E.L., & Reinhard, K. (2005) *The neighbor.* Chicago: University of Chicago Press.

Undermining Surfaces: Tracing the Psychological Significance of Arche in Archetypal Psychology

Rex Olson

In *Archetypal Psychology: A Brief Account,* James Hillman inaugurates archetypal psychology as a radical extension of Jung's analytical psychology. Whereas Jung's work offers a deeper alternative to modern scientific psychology, identifying archetypes as the transcendental ground of psychology, Hillman advances archetypal psychology as a broader, more encompassing perspective, one that recognizes art, culture, and virtually all forms of human activity as originating in the phenomena of the image itself (1983, p.1). Yet both thinkers lay claim to the psychological as dwelling somewhere in the "depths of soul." Hillman distinguishes his work from Jung by articulating a difference between Jung's notion of *archetype* as a noumenal construction, an independent "object" that transcends individual consciousness in the form of the "collective unconscious," and, by contrast, his view of image as an *archetypal* phenomenon, intended to establish, in a real sense, the ontological foundation for archetypal psychology. What amounts to a nominal shift from "archetype" (noun) to "archetypal" (adjective) is meant to correlate with an epistemological turn away from Kantian idealism toward an ontology that locates soul in the world (1983, p. 3).

So instead of descending the depths of the inner personal Self, Hillman looks to find soul in the world, to "read each event for 'something deeper'," exploring the nuance and complexity of images in our relationships with others and between things (1975, p. 29). With this, Hillman claims that he takes the "depth" metaphor of archetypal psychology more seriously than Jung by not taking it "literally."[1] Which is to say, he means to take it metaphorically, for only by seeing the metaphor in things, he argues, can we catch sight of the psychological. For Hillman the work of being psychological can be found in the images of things as they appear, yet at the same time, the image itself emerges as a touchstone of "depth" in our being psychological enough to find it. At issue is whether Hillman can truly succeed in being more psychological than Jung at the moment he claims to be treating the question of metaphor more seriously. Doubtless, Hillman's metaphorical move is pivotal in that it raises the foundational questions that are central for understanding archetypal psychology: namely, to what extent does Hillman's reading of Jung on the question of *arche* or *archi*

---

[1] The fantasy of hidden depths ensouls the world and fosters imagining ever deeper into things. Depth—rather than a literal or physical location—is a primary metaphor necessary for psychological thinking (1983, p. 30).

(origin, source, or first cause) allow archetypal psychology to arrive at a more "in depth" understanding of psyche? And second, at the same time and on a different level, in what way might Hillman's critical appropriation of Jung's text resist exploring the "surface" of images for fear of not being psychological enough? This paper seeks to elucidate the relationship between archetypal psychology's architectonic metaphor, "depth," and the meaning of the psychological as situated in Hillman's text on Jung.

Depth as Psychological

Hillman predicates his view of archetypal psychology on a passage in Jung's essay, "The Practical Use of Dream Analysis," in which Jung quarrels with Freud over the value of free-association for understanding the context of any given dream and its implications for psychotherapy. In response to Freud, Jung argues against "the false belief that the dream is a mere façade concealing the true meaning." "The 'manifest' dream picture," Jung argues, "is the dream itself and contains the whole meaning of the dream" (p. 149). Jung continues:

> What Freud calls the 'dream-façade' is the dreams' obscurity, and this is really only a projection of our own lack of understanding. We say that the dream has a false front only because we fail to see into it. We would do better to say that we are dealing with something like a *text* that is unintelligible not because it has a façade—a *text* has no façade—but simply because we cannot read it. We do not have to get behind such a *text* but must first learn to read it. (p. 149) (italics mine)

By positing the dream as an "unintelligible *text*," Jung questions the extent to which Freud's method of free association effectively deciphers the meaning of a dream. He argues, in fact, that while free association may do well to uncover psychological complexes, it falls short of understanding the significance of a dream or what a dream might mean for the dreamer. For Jung the question of a dream's meaning pushes the critical edge in Freud's thinking beyond the identification of complexes to a "deeper," more psychological level. Writes Jung, "to understand the dream's meaning *I must stick as close as possible to the dream images*," and by inference he intends to stick to the psychological dimension of dreamwork that resides in the meaning we make of our dreams (p. 149) (italics mine). Whereas Jung distinguished between personal and archetypal images, the latter interpreted as being primordial symbols of the psyche, Hillman erases this difference to focus on the image itself. Every image, for Hillman, embodies a particular archetypal value, and every appearance of an image manifests as an expression and measure of psychological life. With Hillman, Jung's notion of "stick to the image"[2] becomes a generalized interpretive strategy that transcends the phenomena of dreams to include the realistic fantasies of our waking lives. It becomes the clarion call and fundamental axiom of archetypal psychology, which makes all psychologies accessible to our understanding.

Now what is curious about this unmistakable, albeit subtle shift, in Jungian thought is the presence of a profound ironic twist. On one side, what counts as a modest extension of Jung's critical method in a desire to go "deeper" shows itself on another side to be closer to the surface of things than what Jung had imagined. To go "deeper" in a psychological sense here means not going as deep in a spatial sense. So if Jung seeks to acknowledge the image as a representation of archetypes, which in and of themselves are unknowable, then Hillman, in taking Jung at his word, works to show how the image in itself is the meaning and ground of our archetypal existence. For both thinkers the meaning of "depth" refers to an ontology of images that seeks to provide a place for the unconscious in expressing what it means to be psychological: the difference lies in the degree to which the notion of *arche* as a root metaphor for both analytical and archetypal psychology entails the act of a critical interpretive stance in relation to the image. Of course each thinker in his own way strives to overcome the Cartesian divide of scientific psychology that virtually denies the existence of the unconscious. But what we discover with Hillman is that, in borrowing Jung's language of "stick to the image," he casts our gaze beyond the Kantian limits of Jungian psychology, beyond images as the phenomena that can reflect the existence of archetypes, to re-locate psyche within the image itself, while at the same time relying on the Kantian motif of immanent critique in order to make that claim possible. The critical difference is that in their hermeneutic understanding of the image Jung is merely Kantian and Hillman, Nietzschean. And in time this difference may be shown to be as significant to depth psychology as the discovery of

---

2 "Stick to the image" (cf. Jung, CW 16, S 320) has become a golden rule of archetypal psychology's method, and this because the image is the primary psychological datum (1983, p. 9).

the quark has been to quantum physics.

Depth as Resistance

In locating psyche in the image, as the ontological ground of and for the psychological, Hillman adopts a hermeneutic phenomenology that respects the inherent play of the image as a *text*. He recognizes that just as the unconscious needs a mind and cannot be construed as the direct object of a "depth" psychology, so too the image, as an expression of psyche, cannot be indirectly glimpsed without understanding its relationship to literal meaning. Like the structure of a Mobius strip, the work of "seeing through" the literal to the metaphorical meaning of a text leads to the realization that the conscious and the unconscious elements of psyche are interconnected and cannot be separated from each other. The spacing between the level of the unconscious signifier and the signified creates a depth in which differing meanings defer to the logocentrism of the text. That is, to the metaphysical presence of the text as image. This might best be illustrated by sharing a dream of a client I once had, J. T., in which he finds himself sitting in the living room of his father's apartment in downtown Manhattan, and while his father is in the kitchen preparing something for them to eat, he notices a book on his father's bookshelf titled "My Giants." The book cover has an image of the New York Giants football team on it and underneath the image, his father's name. What puzzled him about the dream was that his father had been deceased for 15 years at the time, and while living he was never a writer. In fact, his father never had much interest in his college education except that it afforded him the opportunity to play sports. "What are you doing alive?" he exclaims in the dream. "I thought you were dead."

Rather than simply dismiss the dream as absurd from the point of view of the rational mind, "seeing through" the image of "My Giants" to its metaphorical level raises questions that prove to be psychologically significant. On a literal level "My Giants" refers to the home team whom father and son supported as fans while living in New York City. But on a deeper level "My Giants" also might suggest an idealized relationship a son has with his father. The father is viewed as a "giant" in the eyes of a son, a son who looks up to his father, and the appearance of the father's image in a dream 15 years after his untimely death, signifies a correlation between authority issues in my client's waking life and the unresolved issue of losing a father/son relationship that did not have a chance to be "worked through" during the natural course of his development. In the dream the figure of "father" is an overdetermined image of "giant" accomplishments in both sport and writing, two areas in my client's life that were highly valued ("My [Other] Giants"). So to say in the dream "I thought you were dead" can refer just as easily to the "father" as a real life figure as it does to the idealized standard of achievement he represented. For the dream also coincided in waking life with my client's experience of writer's block in his efforts to pen a successful thesis. It was an all too familiar (of family) reminder of my client feeling as though he could not "measure up" as an author to his father's accomplishments on the field as an athlete.

Although archetypal psychology does well to "see through" the literal to the metaphorical, whether in identifying the image or gods or metaphors lurking in the midst of a rational discourse, the psychological for Hillman finds its home in the relationship between singular and multiple dimensions of meaning, in the latent images of the "literal." The maxim "stick to the image," however, leaves an uneraseable trace of an archetype in every image such that it comes to be present as an archetypal image. But if we are to take Heidegger's work seriously, then the appearance of metaphor as archetypal is at the same time a metaphysical presence (Heidegger, 1984/1957), and this can only mean that at the moment in which Hillman claims to be psychological in a self-critical way his text resists the possibility of such a reading. Or to put it differently, his text reflects a moment of psychological resistance at the precise moment his efforts seek to stake out images as being the property and discipline of archetypal psychology. The root metaphor, *arche*, therefore, is not a trace as such, but a full presence, a sense of soul, an image or god that defines the focus and depth of the work in archetypal psychology.

"Depth" as Archi-trace

So we discover that by pushing Hillman's thought to its imaginal limits, his interpretation of psychological life as images of a text, in the end, resists being able to read the text of the image. His work of "seeing through" the literal to the metaphorical meaning of a text is in itself a metaphysical appropriation of the text as if the *text* were a mere repository of images to be disclosed, and this can be seen on a different level as a form of psychological resistance to reading the *text* itself.[3] Here the origin and end of the image, the archi-trace of archetypal psychology, is mediated by the text his interpretation fails to acknowledge for fear of losing sight of the image amid the "surface" structure of words[4]. While the archi-trace reflects the presence of a self-critical moment in archetypal psychology, the *text* that goes unread calls for an additional critical step that would erase the metaphysical presence of the archi-trace to inscribe it otherwise as the trace of a trace[5]. The archi-trace as we know it comes into being if and only if its presence has been placed under erasure: thus leaving a trace of a trace, an irreducible double, a double inscription that undoes the logocentrism of the law of non-contradiction so that temporality is no longer granted organizational priority over spatiality. The arche-trace metaphor would then appear as writings that betray the psychological in signifying twists and turns as something other than meaningful images. The *text*, when read, is death to an image. Hillman seems to worry that such critical work belongs more to the field of postmodern French thought in which deconstructive readings of a text would skip along the surface of words like a water bug, quite apart from the "depth" psychological interpretation he means to claim for archetypal psychology[6]. Nevertheless, if Hillman were to take the next critical step he would have to be engaged in the act of reading a text the way that Derrida might, and that would risk taking his project out of the psychological depths he seeks to preserve as the territory of archetypal psychology. In as much as Hillman may seek to distance himself from the French version of deconstruction, he seems content to arrive at a deconstructive "depth" psychology that has no bottom, no absolute "end," except that which he finds in an "infinite" play

---

[3] Note that in the passage Hillman cites regarding "stick to the image," Jung states "a *text* has no façade—but simply because we cannot read it. We do not have to get behind such a *text* but must first learn to read it." Hillman spent his career teaching how psychologizing is a way of reading. But the text he claims to read may exceed the limits of his imaginal grasp.

[4] "Moving from outside in, it is a process of *interiorizing*; moving from the process the surface of visibilities to the less visible, it is a process of deepening; . . . " (1975, p. 140).

[5] See "Freud and the Scene of Writing" for a discussion of the phenomenon of archi-trace in Freud's work as functioning something like the old Mystic Writing Pad.

[6] Hillman's treatment of metaphor as a response to Heidegger's blurring of the boundaries between philosophy and literature in *The Principle of Reason* may have been a sincere effort to try and hedge off French deconstruction. After all it is no secret that Heidegger's later works had a significant influence on the contemporary French intelligentsia responsible for much of its translation and reception in France. See in particular Derrida's "White Mythology: Metaphor in the Text of Philosophy" and "The Retrait of Metaphor."

of meaning from the image, where meanings of the image come into being as the ultimate ends of psyche.

By insisting that we "stick to the image" Hillman offers a hermeneutic phenomenology that undermines the surface layers of *text* in search of images and meaningful experiences that he claims discloses the psychological. Such is the unwitting metaphysical work of finding Hermes in the stone[7]. Yet the power of Hillman's thinking seems to lie more in the critical work of "sticking" to the (text of the) image than to the culmination of that work as an image. What gets overlooked and forgotten is *how* the force of his radical critique gives meaning and place to the psychological, that the psychological may well find itself in the radical force of his critique more so than in any image of it. And this, finally, leaves us with an image of Hillman, who like the trickster figure Bre'er Rabbit in the old Uncle Remus stories of the South, can be viewed as mired in the textual goo of his archetypal tar baby. The more he struggles to free himself from the *text*, the more mired in its goo he becomes. It is not until he accepts the fate of his near death situation that he tricks us one last time: Hillman with Bre'er Rabbit at home in the briar patch, laughing their asses off.

References

Aristotle (1980). *The metaphysics*. (H. Tredennick, Trans.). Cambridge: Harvard University Press.

Derrida, J. (1978). Freud and the scene of writing. In *Writing and difference*. (A. Bass, Trans.). (pp. 196-231). Chicago: The University of Chicago Press. (Original work published 1967).

Derrida, J. (1978). The retrait of metaphor. *Enclitic*, 2, 5-33.

Derrida, J. (1982). White mythology: metaphor in the text of philosophy. In *Margins* (A. Bass, Trans.) (pp. 29-67). Chicago: The University of Chicago Press.

Heidegger, M. (1984). *The principle of reason*. (R. Lilly, Trans.). Bloomington: Indiana University Press. (Original work published 1957).

Hillman, J. (1975). *Re-visioning psychology*. New York: Harper & Row Publishers.

Hillman, J. (1983). *Archetypal psychology: a brief account*. Dallas: Spring Publications Inc.

Jung, C. G. (1966). *The practice of psychotherapy: essays on the psychology of the transference and other subjects*. (R. F. C. Hull, Trans.). In Bolligen Series, 16, sec. 320 Princeton: Princeton University Press.

---

[7] Cf. Aristotle book V of his *Metaphysics* in which he briefly describes "Hermes in the stone" as the relation of the potential to the actual existence in things as "soul is the cause of being an animal" (p. 239).

Technology – Textuality – Virtuality

Eva-Maria Simms

In the early 1980's I was Robert Romanyshyn's assistant as he was writing *Technology as Symptom and Dream* (Romanyshyn, 1989), and I spent many hours in the library looking through books on medieval and renaissance art to find images that illustrate the psychological changes in the 15th century world. Romanyshyn's work gave me the framework for studying history as a psychologist and to look for the traces of how the world we experience today has come about. It taught me to look for the markers of the different meaning structures by which people in the past have interpreted and understood their worlds. It instilled in me a profound suspicion of the contemporary concepts and tools with which we think.

One of our most fundamental, cherished, and taken for granted intellectual tools is the written text. In three earlier essays I have tried to tackle the phenomenology and metabletics of literacy (Simms, 2008a, 2008b, 2010) in order to understand how reading and "bookishness", to use Illich's term (1996), alter human consciousness in Western history, but also in the life of every child who learns to read. I want to return to this topic and think through textuality as an event that is not *natural* but *technological*, and which functions as a symptom and dream in our culture – perhaps even as its symptom and dream *par excellence*.

How Technology Works

The word 'technology' is generally defined as the application of tools and methods, particularly the study, development, and application of devices, machines, and techniques for manufacturing and productive processes. On a deeper level, however, technology is the disclosure and manipulation of the essence of things (Heidegger, 1993). In a lecture at Duquesne University the social critic Ivan Illich described briefly the way technology works: technologies extract the essences out of human abilities by instrumentalizing them and by reducing or eliminating their original lived context. An example is the invention of the automobile: the essential ability of human movement is extracted and intensified through the technology of the car, which in turn reduces the lived and embodied context of human motility. According to Illich, when human experience becomes technologized, a double process of *intensification* of some experiential elements and the *de-contextualization and reduction* of others can be observed. I have found Illich's principle of intensification and de-contextualization as the two operational functions of technological processes extremely helpful in analyzing the impact technologies have on human experience.

It is not customary to think of the written text as a technological implement, but I want to show in the following that literacy is actually a technology which intensifies and de-contextualizes particular aspects of perceptual consciousness. Illich and Sanders (1988) have argued that alphabetization, i.e. the translation of the phonetic sound system into visual alphabetic notation, is an epistemological practice with far-reaching impact on mind and culture. Illich (1996, p. 5) has traced the creation of the "bookish" mind to the monastic reading and writing tradition of the 12th century, which built the foundation for new thinking practices, the founding of schools and universities, and the dissemination of ideas through the printing press in the following centuries. The invention of pervasive literacy, as Postman (1994) has argued, has changed what people think about (the stuff in books), talk about (ideas that are removed from the present situation), how they think (in linear, logical ways) and what they value (education). In literate cultures those who cannot read cannot participate in the cultural commerce of their culture. Hence children are set aside from adult life in educational reservations where their consciousnesses are restructured by intensive literacy training until they "graduate" and are allowed to share in adult activities. Reading is a technology that changes the structure of human consciousness. Textuality is a *consciousness technology*: it alters the very way we perceive, think, and believe in what is real.

The Phenomenology of Reading: the Magic of Synesthesia

In his phenomenological analysis of alphabetization as a perceptual phenomenon, Abram (1996) shows how perception changes in the transition from oral to textual engagement with the world in non-literate, animistic cultures. His analysis, however, also applies to the restructuring child consciousness undergoes in the transition from orality to literacy. Prior to the immersion into textuality, the creative, *synesthetic* interplay of the senses with the perceived world creates a sense of magical envelopment. The earth is experienced as alive and meaningful and full of messages to the perceiver. Prereflective perception is synesthetic, participatory, and animistic. Synesthesia works by bringing all the senses into play in the act of perception (Merleau-Ponty, 1962). We see something and know what sound it will make when we knock on it, how its texture should feel to the touching fingers, or how heavy it is when we pick it up. Even very young infants have this ability of cross-modal, synesthetic perception (Meltzoff & Borton, 1979; Stern, 1985). When one sensory mode is evoked the others come into play as well. When we learn how to read, however, "we must break the spontaneous participation of our eyes and our ears in the surrounding terrain (where they had ceaselessly converged in the synesthetic encounter with animals, plants, and streams) in order to recouple those senses upon the flat surface of the page"(Abram, 1996, p. 131).

Abram's analysis of the relationship between alphabetization and perception makes clear that the magical synesthesia, the evocation of all the senses, is relocated from the world to the text. When the eye perceives something, the other senses participate, even if they do not perceive directly. *This is the virtual, imaginary dimension of perception* (Merleau-Ponty, 1962). As the eyes read through the signs on the page, the mind brings all the senses into play to create a whole virtual world complete with sensory resonances. The magical power of books has its roots in the phenomenon of synesthesia: as we read, the world of the book is as compelling and sometimes more real to us than the actual world of the senses. "As nonhuman animals, plants, and even 'inanimate' rivers once spoke to our tribal ancestors, so the 'inert' letters on the page now speak to us! This is a form of animism that we take for granted, but it is animism none the less – as mysterious as a talking stone" (p. 131). And Abram is correct: we are animists when it comes to textual signification. We give ourselves over to the mysterious voices and beings that arise through the letters on the page and take them seriously – and among literate people we take the world of texts more seriously than the world of the senses: most children spend more time in the text centered symbolic discourse of school than in exploring and talking about the world they directly perceive; most adults spend the majority of their time dealing with textual matters such as e-mails, files, books, news, intellectual ideas, facebook, websites, which all co-opt the natural synesthesia of the body and eliminate attention to the world of the senses.

The introduction of literacy changes children's relationship to the world because it shifts their attention from the animated, meaningful context of their perceived worlds toward the purely virtual and *unperceived* dimension of the text's virtual world. Abram argues that the magic of full, synesthetic perception, the spell that it casts upon us and the force with which it draws us into a connection with the world, has changed its direction when we enter a literate world. Literacy is a technology that distances us from the life world and dulls our ability to attend to and "read" fully the expressions of the world of minerals, plants, animals and the elements: "it is only when a culture shifts its participation to these printed letters that the stones fall silent" (Abram, 1996, p. 131). Here we witness one of the structural intensifications and reductions which are the hallmarks of technology: chirographic technology *reduces* the body's perceptual engagement with a plentiful, signifying, sensory environment and *intensifies* the virtual/symbolic dimension of language through manipulating synesthesia.

The Phenomenology of Reading: Entering a Text

In his phenomenological analysis of the literary work of art, Ingarden (1973) points out that out of the component parts of textuality (phonemes, words, sentences, and the textual unfolding as a whole) a particular *world* arises, and it is this world (which transcends the author's intended meaning) which the reader finds compelling – or not. The reader has to be able to "climb aboard" and "accept the given perspectives" (Iser, 1972, p. 282), while at the same time be willing to collaborate with the text to allow it to come to fruition in the imagination.

The world displayed by the text is a product of what Merleau-Ponty's calls "the organism of words" (1962, p. 182), which creates a new dimension of experience alongside the perceptual world. The reader's imagination fills the gaps in the text and supplies what is not there. The text, on the other hand, allows the reader to live and experience worlds that could never come to his or her immediate, embodied senses. The virtual dimension, as Iser points out, lies in the engagement between mind and text and is created through the interaction between consciousness and chirographic material.

Virtuality, as we saw before, is an essential constituent of synesthesia: we see a red dress, but we also virtually assume the softness of its texture or the weight of its fabric without ever touching it. Perception itself has a virtual dimension which weaves sense perceptions into a coherent whole and which functions as a present absence. The virtual dimension of textual technology *intensifies* this sense of present absence and drags consciousness along in its wake by promising it a coherent, satisfying world. But it is a world that leaves our senses behind. The absent becomes more real than the present.

A book takes on its full existence only in its readers (Poulet, 1969). They absorb new experiences, but at a price: "As soon as I replace my direct perception by the words of a book, I deliver myself, bound hand and foot to the omnipotence of fiction. I say farewell to what is, in order to feign belief in what is not. I surround myself with fictitious beings; I become the prey of language. There is no escaping this take-over. Language surrounds me with its unreality" (p.55). The reader's thoughts and feelings are occupied by the thoughts of the author, and these in their turn draw new boundaries in our personality. The consciousness of the reader "behaves as though it were the consciousness of another" and "on loan to another" who feels, suffers, and thinks in it (p. 56-57).

Here we have another intensification and reduction of language practice: the possibility of thinking according to others (when we listen to them) is *intensified* in the monological exposure to the text's voice and in the *reduction* of the reader's own speech. Reading requires the sustained immersion in the fictional world created by an author. The silence of the reader and the temporal structure of the continuous, uninterrupted voice of the author preclude the reader from interjecting and changing the direction of the language exchange. The world of the book worms its way into the consciousness of the reader. All a reader can do is close the book and refuse participation in the symbolic world the text promises.

The Phenomenology of Reading: Virtuality and the Reproduction of Culture

In oral conversations, children take up each other's thoughts and spin them on and send them back and forth. In textuality, however, others thought processes, memories, and images are recapitulated and accomplished in the child's mind without the child's direct, embodied response. Silencing the back and forth of embodied conversations intensifies the reader's exposure to the author's thoughts, images, and feelings. The most significant change that literacy introduces is the amplification of virtual realities in the minds of children. As soon as children cross over the threshold of alphabetic decoding, they enter a compelling wonderland of ideas and experiences *which are not their own*, but which powerfully shape the mind. Literate cultures know that they need this virtual world and that they have to colonize it. I call the reality which is created by textuality *the virtual order*. By replicating the virtual order in the minds of children, on a massive scale, literate cultures reproduce themselves over the generations by establishing canons of texts that have to be read and internalized by children. Cultural memory is transmitted by texts. We call this process "education". Education, by intensifying the virtual, is engaged in a massive repression and restructuring of embodied perception.

We can get a better view of the significance of the virtual order when we look at it from a cultural-historical perspective. Literate cultures have commerce in the realities that are created by texts: books hold knowledge and cultural memory. Books (and electronic media today) are a storehouse for memories of all sorts—records of legal transactions, historical events, philosophical argument, poetry, scientific inventions and ideas, religious texts and commentaries, maps and calendars. Book content is the cultural currency that is transferred in the conversations of literate people and determines the intellectual and moral climate. Mumford argues that the invention of the printing press and the ensuing spread of writing technology led to a radical transformation of Western culture. "More than any other device, the printed book released people from the domination of the immediate and the local.... print made a greater impression than the actual events....To exist was to exist in print: the rest of the world tended gradually to become more shadowy. Learning became book learning" (Mumford, 1934, p. 28).

Books do not merely contain information, but structure the way we think about reality. Literacy makes it possible to erect a conceptual scaffold above our everyday experience, which then is disseminated and transmitted through the authority of media and education. This makes the virtual reality of texts believable and compelling, even if it contradicts our senses: *to exist is to exist in print*. The immediate and local experience has been sacrificed to the virtual dimension of texts.

On their way into the adult virtual order we ask each child to make a series of sacrifices in order to become literate: bodies do not lie on the floor or skip through the streets but must sit in rows; the speech of friends is forbidden and re-defined as idle chatter; the magic of the sense-world is drained until it becomes dulled and distant, like the flat piece of sky beyond the sealed classroom window.

Where once an enduring house was
A conceptual structure proposes itself, at odds with everything,
Belonging completely to thinking, as if it still stood in the brain.
(R.M. Rilke, 7th Duino Elegy [1966], my translation)

References

Abram, D. (1996). *The spell of the sensuous.* New York: Vintage Books.
Heidegger, M. (1993). The question concerning technology. In D. F. Krell (Ed.), *Basic writings.* San Francisco: HarperCollins Publishers.
Illich, I. (1996). *In the vineyard of the text: A commentary to Hugh's Didascalicon.* Chicago: University of Chicago Press.
Illich, I., & Sanders, B. (1988). *ABC: The alphabetization of the popular mind.* San Francisco: North Point Press.
Ingarden, R. (1973). *The literary work of art* (G. G. Grabowicz, Trans.). Evanston, IL:

Northwestern University Press.

Iser, W. (1972). The reading process: a phenomenological approach. *New Literary History*, *3*(2), 279-299.

Meltzoff, A. N., & Borton, W. (1979). Intermodal matching by neonates. *Nature*, *282*, 403-404.

Merleau-Ponty, M. (1962). *Phenomenology of perception* (C. Smith, Trans.). London: Routledge & Kegan Paul Ltd.

Mumford, L. (1934). *Technics and civilization*. New York: Harcourt, Brace & Co.

Postman, N. (1994). *The disappearance of childhood*. New York: Vintage Books.

Poulet, G. (1969). Phenomenology of reading. *New Literary History*, *1*(1), 53-68.

Rilke, R. M. (1966). *Werke, 3 vols*. Frankfurt am Main: Insel Verlag.

Romanyshyn, R. D. (1989). *Technology as symptom and dream*. London: Routledge.

Simms, E. M. (2008a). *The child in the world: Embodiment, time, and language in early childhood*. Detroit: Wayne State University Press.

Simms, E. M. (2008b). Literacy and the appearance of childhood. *Janus Head*, *10*(2), 445-459.

Simms, E. M. (2010). Questioning the value of literacy: A phenomenology of speaking and reading in children. In K. Coats (Ed.), *Handbook of Children's and Young Adult Literature*. London/New York: Routledge.

Stern, D. N. (1985). *The interpersonal world of the infant: A view from psychoanalysis and developmental psychology*. New York: Basic Books, Inc.

Ethos Anthropoi Daimon and the
Ethical Character of Romanyshyn's Psychology

Michael P. Sipiora

Introduction

In his contribution to a Festschrift for J.H. van den Berg, Robert Romanyshyn (1985) identifies several "psychological themes" (p. 100) inherent in his teacher's ingenious metabletic phenomenology, the last of which is that of an ethical psychology.[1] I believe this theme is as important to Romanyshyn's work as it is that of van den Berg. Insofar as Romanyshyn's thinking is informed by both phenomenological philosophy and depth psychology, we will pursue the notion of ethics from both these orientations. Consideration of a saying from Heraclitus, *Ethos anthropoi daimon* (B 119), provides an opportunity to do just that and thus affords a perspective from which to appreciate the ethical character of Romanyshyn's work. This fragment is one of the oldest and most discussed texts in the Western tradition. A short saying—"only three words" as the philosopher Martin Heidegger (1977) notes in his "Letter on Humanism" (p. 256), "three little words," as the psychologist James Hillman (1996) refers to them in his *The Soul's Code* (p. 256)—that has invited countless interpretations. It is both an aporia that entangles reflection and a vortex that provokes imagination.

I. Heidegger

> Soon after *Being and Time* appeared a young friend asked me, "When are you going to write an ethics?"
>
> Heidegger (1977, p. 255)

Near the end of his "Letter on Humanism," in which Heidegger (1977) critiques various humanisms for not setting the essence of the human "high enough" (p. 233), he refers to Heraclitus. According to Heidegger, Fragment 119 "says something so simply that from it the essence of the *ethos* immediately comes to light" (p. 256). But in order to bring that essence into view, we have to refuse the usual translation and attempt to

---

[1] These themes were central to my reflection on metabletics as a conscientious psychology (1999). In that essay I conclude by referring to both Romanyshyn's understanding of an ethical psychology and Heidegger's Heraclitus inspired notion that ethics ponders the dwelling of mortals (p. 44).

understand the fragment in a Greek way. Thus Heidegger takes *ethos* as "dwelling place," *diamon* as "the god," and *anthropoi* as "what belongs to man in his essence" leading to: "Man dwells, insofar as he is man, in the nearness of god" (p. 256).

A story mentioned by Aristotle is offered as amplification. The story recounts a group of "strangers" who come upon Heraclitus hoping to catch him in thought but instead finding him merely warming himself.[2] In response to their "consternation," he calls to them: "For here too the gods are present" (p. 256). Heidegger comments:

> *Kai entautha*, "even here," at the stove, in the ordinary place where every thing and every condition, each deed and thought is intimate and commonplace, that is, familiar [*geheuer*], "even there" in the sphere of the familiar, *einai theous*, it is the case that "the gods come to presence". (p. 258)

Returning to the fragment, Heidegger now renders: "The (familiar) abode for man is the open region for the presencing of god (the unfamiliar one)" (p. 258). What is then implied is that "'ethics,' in keeping with the basic meaning of the word *ethos*, should now say that 'ethics' ponders the abode of man" (p. 258). Thus Heidegger asserts that the "original ethics" is "... that thinking which thinks the truth of Being as the primordial element of man, as one who ek-sists." (p. 258)

Yet such thinking is ontology rather than ethics, or rather neither ontology nor ethics because more fundamental than either as it "defines man's essential abode from Being and toward Being" (p. 259). This "original" way of thinking ethics leads to dwelling: "the jointure of Being fatefully enjoins the essence of man to dwell in the truth of Being" (p. 259-60). So it is that Heidegger can claim: "Hölderlin's verse, 'Full of merit, yet poetically, man dwells on this earth' is no adornment of thinking that rescues itself from science by means of poetry" (p. 260). *Ethos*, our familiar place as human, is poetic dwelling.

---

[2] Compare Krell's (1992) interpretation in *Daimon life: Heidegger and life-philosophy*, pp. 1-5.

Each person enters the world called.
Hillman (1996, p. 7)

Heraclitus' Fragment 119 appears as a section title in Hillman's (1996) *The Soul's Code,* a book about personal callings, a "sense of fate," and the "power of character" (pp. 3-4). Hillman notes the "frequent render[ing of Fragment 119] as 'Character is fate'" (p. 256) and lists nine other English translations before offering his own interpretation. "The *daimon* part is easy enough," he notes,

> for we have already accepted the translation of daimon as genius (Latin) and then transposed it into more modern terms such as "angel," "soul," "paradigm," "image," "fate," "inner twin," "acorn," "life companion," "guardian," "heart's calling." (p. 257)

Hillman had introduced the *daimon* at the very beginning of the book, not in reference to Heraclitus but rather to Plato in the context of the Myth of Er that provides the overarching narrative for Hillman's "Acorn Theory." According to this theory, we are accompanied through life by diamon who carries knowledge of our chosen (by the soul before birth) but now forgotten (as we come into life and live out our) fate. Hillman is keen to point out that just as Plato takes his myths seriously but not literally, we do well to do the same. The diamon is not to be taken literally as a measurable fact or environmental factor but the need to take it seriously is confirmed by the critical observation that while all cultures seem to have a sense of it—referring to it with multiple names—it is utterly absent from our modern western view, psychology in particular. The diamon references the total "other" that appears in our lives and lays claim upon our living.

As for *ethos,* Hillman advises: "If we 'strip away the ethics' [in the sense of the "moralism of Hebrew, Roman, Christian religiosity" (p. 259] from *ethos,* we find it carries more the meaning of 'habit'" (p. 259). *Ethos* then refers to one's "habitual way of life" (Peters, 1967, p. 66). It is those ways of relating and engaging that typify, characterize one's living. In "the realism of Heraclitus: You are how you are. 'How' is the crucial term, which links life as it is habitually 'behaved' with the call of your image" (Hillman, p. 259). Character, as he develops this pre-modern notion, is "the aesthetic style of lasting traits expressed in individualized tastes and behaviors" (1999, pp. xix-xxx), that issues from the call of your image, carried and remember by the diamon.

From here, Hillman (1996) makes one of his trademark moves.

> Though Heraclitus connects character (*ethos*) and human ethics directly with the diamon, it is *its* fate that becomes our concern. The egocentric focus of humanism makes us believe that the diamon, having chosen us to inhabit, concerns itself with our fate. But what about *its* fate? (p. 260)

In his archetypal perspective, the deepest parts of who are, for Hillman, are what is most "not us" but which lays claim on us and in so doing grants us our uniqueness. It would be misguided—the mistake of humanism—to identify this claim with the ego. Attention to the diamon is a concern for what animates our habitual way of life. "The daimon then," Hillman concludes,

> becomes the source of human ethics, and the happy life—what the Greeks called *eudaimonia*—is the life that is good for the daimon. Not only does it bless us with its calling, we bless it with our style of following. (p. 260)

Character, *ethos*, is the "cluster of characteristics" (Hillman, 1999, p. 197) evoked by the claim of the daimon.

III Convergences

It is not surprising that both Heidegger's and Hillman's interpretations of Heraclitus lead to their matters of greatest concern—Heidegger's thinking of being and Hillman's imagining of soul. What will interest us here is how they both do so in terms of the same three (mere/little) words of Heraclitus. There are several intriguing points of convergence between Heidegger's and Hillman's interpretations. First, they both critique humanism. For Heidegger (1977), the metaphysical character of humanism mistakes the essence of the human by failing to recognize that "man essentially occurs in his essence, where he is claimed by Being" (p. 227). On his side, Hillman faults humanisms for their egocentrism and accompanying obliviousness to the diamon's calling. Second, both Hillman and Heidegger emphasize that it is not us but the fate of what claims us that we need to attend —for Heidegger the juncture of Being [*Ereignis*], for Hillman the diamon. Third, they both focus on habit, inhabiting, and dwelling. And finally, fourth, there is Heidegger's reference to poetic dwelling and Hillman's related notion of aesthetic style.

IV Response-ability

Turning to Romanyshyn (1985), his remarks on the ethical dimension of van den Berg's work continue upon his previously having shown that as a "cultural therapeutics, metabletic phenomenology invites and even forces us to remember that what we experience is also a way of experiencing" (p. 105). The "consequence," as he sees it, is that "we as humanity are responsible for what we see and say" (p. 105). Paying heed to the prophetic visions of William Blake and Mary Shelly leads to the recognition that the technological world is the incarnation of our shared linear perspective style of vision. It is to this vision, our world, which we need be able to respond.

> [W]e need a psychology that enables us to respond, which restores our sense of responsibility. We need a psychology that in its therapeutic dimension restores humanity to its place on earth. (p. 106)

This notion of ethics—as involving the ability or capacity to respond to what claims us—that he identifies in van den Berg's metabletics, permeates Romanyshyn's own work.

Of the many ways in which one could relate the earlier noted convergences in interpreting Heraclitus to Romanyshyn's work, I will focus on these: the notion of us as figures-in-stories upon which his understanding of psychological life is based; the ethical epistemology that is at the heart of his "alchemical hermeneutic" research method, the persistent theme of the body, and the relationship with the poets that pervades his writings.

In relation to the first convergence, Romanyshyn's way of taking human being is informed by both the phenomenological and depth psychological critiques of humanism. His understanding of the human emerges from his conception of psychological life as a metaphorical reality of reflection lived in and through the cultural world. In his first book, *Psychological Life from Science to Metaphor*, he asserts: "To meet psychological life on its own terms requires a respect for the figures who are one's psychological life" (1982, p. 17). This understanding of our psychological life as figures in stories is informed by Heidegger's notion of our essence as ek-sistence. It is as figures-in-stories that we exist psychologically. The emphasis on figures—plural—rather than a focus on the singular person, is aligned with Hillman's rejection of an egocentric focus as well as congruent with his understanding of character as characters, a "cluster of characteristics" (Hillman, 1999, p. 197).

Romanyshyn' (2007) notion of an "ethical epistemology," which is at the heart of his alchemical hermeneutic research method, attempts "to make a place for the unconscious in our ways of knowing the world" (p. 336) by acknowledging and giving voice to the researcher's "unconscious complex presence to the work" (p. 341). This epistemology relates to the second convergence, in which Heidegger and Hillman attend to what claims us, by accepting, in Romanyshyn's words, "that one has been called into the work through one's complexes for the sake of being the agent of the work itself" (p. 344) and ultimately in service to what he portrays as the "unfinished business" of the "ancestors" (p. 341).

We can relate the third convergence—habit, inhabiting, and dwelling—to Romanyshyn's sustained attention to the body. The repression of the gestural, lived-body, the mortal body that dwells on the earth, is a central concern in his book *Technology as Symptom and Dream*. The gestural body figures prominently in Romanyshyn's writing on therapy where he repeatedly contends that "all therapy is body work" and that the transference relationship is enacted in the gestural field. Closely related to character, the gestural body, as Romanyshyn portrays it, re-sponds to what Hillman (1996) noted as "the call of the image" (p. 259).

Romanyshyn's (2002) musing in so many of the essays in *Ways of the Heart* relate to the forth convergence by highlight both his dialogue with the poets—Rilke, Elliot, Blake, Keats, and Cummings, "all shadowed by the ghost of Orpheus" (p. 85)—and his cultivation of an "aesthetic sensibility." (p. 132). He says "the poets have been my preferred companions for more than the thirty years that I have been a psychologist" (p. 120). Echoing Heidegger's (1977) remark concerning Hölderlin's verse, that it "no adornment of thinking that rescues itself from science by means of poetry" (p. 260), Romanyshyn (2002) declares: 'it is more appropriate that that the psychologist be a failed poet than a good scientist" (p. 123). Connecting both the poetry and aesthetics, and providing the reason that the psychologist is better a poet then a fact-finding scientist, is the metaphorical character of psychological life.

In conclusion, led by interpretations of Heraclitus' *Ethos anthropoi daimon*, we can glean the ethical character of Romanyshyn's psychology. In his vision of our psychological life, we dwell as gestural figures responsive and responsible to the call of ancestral stories that animate our psychological life. Speaking of the imaginal approach that he has developed in the "space between the two traditions of phenomenology...and depth psychology" (2002, p. xix), Romanyshyn writes:

> Action, including language, is drawn out of us in response to what has addressed us, and in this respect gives presence and voice to what is otherwise silent or forgotten. The symptom in the event, the symbol in the idea, the fantasy in the fact, the dream in the institutional structure, are brought from darkness into visibility. In this regard, the one who acts, including the one who speaks, is a witness for the unspoken, one who, in being responsive to being addressed, is response-able. Action, including language, in-formed by the imaginal perspective, is therefore essentially ethical. (p. xxii)

References

Heidegger, M. (1977). Letter on humanism. (F.A. Capuzzi and J.G. Gray, Trans.). In D. F. Krell (Ed.), *Martin Heidegger's basic writings* (pp. 193-242). New York: Harper and Row.

Hillman, J. (1996). *The soul's code: In search of character and calling.* New York: Warner Books.

Hillman, J. (1999). *The force of character and the lasting life.* New York: Ballantine Books.

Krell, D.F. (1992). *Daimon life: Heidegger and life-philosophy.* Bloomfield, IN: Indiana University Press.

Peters, E.F. (1967). *Greek philosophical terms: A historical lexicon.* New York: New York University Press.

Romanyshyn, R. (1982). *Psychological life: From science to metaphor.* Austin: University of Texas Press.

Romanyshyn, R. (1985). The despotic eye. In D. Kruger, (Ed.), *The changing reality of modern man* (pp. 87-109). Pittsburgh: Duquesne University Press.

Romanyshyn, R. (1989). *Technology as symptom and dream.* New York: Routledge.

Romanyshyn, R. (2002). *Ways of the heart: Essays toward an imaginal psychology.* Pittsburgh: Trivium Publications.

Romanyshyn, R. (2007). *The wounded researcher.* New Orleans: Spring Journal Books.

Sipiora, M.P. (1999) Obligations beyond competence: Metablectics as a conscientious. *In Metablectics: J.H. van den Berg's historical phenomenology,* (pp. 29-46). Pittsburgh: Simon Silverman Phenomenology Center

Psychological
Reflections

An Honored Guest in the iMfolozi, and the Possibility of Homecoming

Roger Brooke

In 1990 Robert Romanyshyn joined me and a small group of five psychologists in the iMfolozi basin in KwaZulu Natal. Our two rangers were experts in wilderness craft, and they had rifles that could drop an elephant if needed. We walked no more than a few miles by day and camped around a small fire by night. We slept in sleeping bags on ground sheets under the night sky. No tents, and we carried everything we needed in backpacks. We took turns through the night keeping a small fire going, brewing coffee for the next night watch, and making ourselves and our shadows dancing in the trees visible to any dangerous game animals in our immediate vicinity. This was lion country--home to "the big five"[1]--and the largest herd of rhino in Africa.

Something that I talked about one evening, but have never written, is what had happened in that place a few years earlier (1986). My group was lead by Dr. Ian Player, his legendary Zulu guide, Magqubu[2] Ntombela. Mr. Ntombela was a traditional healer as well as a guide, born in the vicinity of the iMfolozi around 1900. For him, every hill, rocky outcrop or living thing had stories to tell. The boundary between the living and the dead was more like a permeable veil than a clear divide. Player had lived much of his life in the iMfolozi since he became a Park Ranger there in 1952. Ntombela had worked there since 1914.

That first night we made camp under a grove of acacia trees. It was the dry season, so the river was mostly a wide area of dry sand with ankle deep stretches of clear water and a few deeper water holes (to be avoided!). The river flowed gently towards us from the south, then turned east before curving around a high ridge about a kilometer off to our left.

I awoke around midnight to the sound of a traditional Zulu community celebration on the ridge along the river. I was surprised to realize that we had camped so close to the edge of the Park, and felt vaguely disappointed that we were not as deep in the wilderness basin as I had thought we were. But I enjoyed the syncopated drum rhythms, singing, occasional shouts, and laughter, cattle bells, floating across to me and my companions, sleeping under the stars around the fire. I lay awake looking at the southern stars and listening to the celebrations, imagining perhaps

---

[1] The "Big Five" are lion, leopard, elephant, rhinoceros, Cape buffalo, but the iMfolozi includes hippo and hyena as well.
[2] The "gq" is pronounced with a sharp click formed by the tongue snapping off the front roof of the upper palate, just behind the front teeth.

a wedding, or the successful birth of a child, or perhaps, the presence of

an honored guest. I propped myself up on an elbow, but could not see any lights on the ridge, silhouetted against the star lit sky. One of my companions was sitting night watch on a log near the perimeter of firelight, tin cup of coffee in hand. I listened to the festivities for perhaps ten minutes before I rolled over, pulled my sleeping bag over my head to soften the noise, and peacefully drifted back to sleep.

At breakfast the following morning I happened to mention the festivities I had heard and received a rather odd look from Player. He translated into Zulu for Ntombela, who looked intensely interested and asked a few questions. Back and forth we went in translation through Player. Finally Ntombela said that I had been given a gift.

Player then explained that we were many miles from the edge of the Park and that nobody had lived on that ridge for a hundred years. Nobody else had heard anything.

The village had been where Ntombela's father had lived, and where spears were forged for King Cetshwayo's Zulu army of 20,000 men that had killed over a thousand British soldiers at Isandlawana not far away on January 22, 1879. Ntombela's father had fought in that battle. The basin in which we camped had been King Shaka's personal hunting grounds. We were as deep in Zulu history as one could be.

I have no idea how to account for that experience. The usual suspects seem possible but silly. Until our conversation that morning, the experience was so matter-of-fact that it had not seemed particularly interesting or significant. Although the sounds were some way off, they were as clear as the cow bells I had heard, and obviously came from that ridge to our east. We were too deep in the park to hear anything from outside it. I had assumed that my companion drinking coffee was enjoying the sounds just as I was. But no-one had heard anything at all, apart from the occasional sounds of the African night.

Player and Ntombela had no doubt that I had been present in some sense to the village celebrations that had taken place a hundred or more years ago. It is the only such experience that I have knowingly had.

I think we should resist calling it an experience of the

"supernatural." The term supernatural assumes that there is a natural world which is objective and governed by the laws of natural science--the science of nature so defined. Anything experienced that cannot be accounted for in these terms is then termed "super"-natural, meaning "above" or "beyond" the natural (Abram, 1996, p. 8). The term assumes terms of reference and explanation that preclude both understanding and explanation.

Jung's (1952) term synchronicity is helpful, but we must be careful to understand that it does not *explain* anything either. For Jung, the term marks out an area of experience that is at once psychic and material, and where these terms are meaningfully rather than causally linked. Synchronicity describes a realm of experience and its material concurrence. As such it opens the door to further reflection and enquiry. It is the first term in a conversation, not an explanatory term that brings conversation to an end. Following Jung's thinking regarding synchronicity, we are encouraged to ask the right question. This is not the question of whether the experience was "real" or a dream. nor is it primarily a question of explanation. The premises of those questions preclude answers. We need, instead, to ask the question of what such an experience might mean to the experiencing person.

My family has a British Colonial history. The British soldiers at Isandlwana were probably wearing Brooke family wool. I was in the heart of the Zulu ancestral home, a Colonial heir and a depth psychologist, guided by a Zulu healer who was heir to a long line of warriors. I remembered how I had lain awake wondering if there had been the arrival of an honored guest. I felt mildly embarrassed at the inflated thought that I might be the honored guest welcomed into that village full of joyful veteran Isandlwana warriors. But I did like to imagine that I was the one being honored with the gift of Zulu hospitality.

I wondered whether Magqubu Ntombela might have wanted me to visit that village that night. He knew that I was interested in the dreams of suffering people, just as he was. It did seem that we shared more that night than we manifestly did by day. We could not speak each other's language, and, as an English speaking white South African under Apartheid, I might as well have been a foreigner.

Except for this: I feel more at home in the African bush than I feel at home anywhere. My life feels complete. Since I am not alone in this experience, let me change "I" to "we". We have no more long term goals there, no commitments, or mortgage to keep up. We have dropped, even though only for a few days, into a world that is not anthropocentric but centered in being, a presence magnificently indifferent to our anxious human concerns. Within this place all is forgiven, but nothing can be taken for granted either. One is merely part of the food chain; in common with other large animals, we are mostly eaten by the tiny things, such as ticks.

Many people who have not spent time in the African wilderness imagine that one would be always on edge. In fact one is simply alert and attentive to what one is doing and to one's surroundings. One cannot live like this, of course, and the Zulu villagers who had lived on that ridge would not have lived their goal directed lives (including planning how to beat the mighty British) continuously in this kind of presence either. We need not value this capacity for presence more than the meaningfully engaged and productive way of being in the world. However, we can affirm the possibility of presence that is granted to us as a celebratory gift, and which is there to sustain us as the ground upon which our everyday lives are figured.

As such a gift, the natural world, with its biodiversity, also makes its ethical claim upon us. Each living thing brings its own kind of intelligence into the world, reflecting both our living communion with it and our human difference (Abram, 2010). If we are moved spiritually when we drop into the iMfolozi basin, as nearly all of us are, we are claimed by that place to bear ethical witness both to it and to all such places--even, perhaps, in our back yards. We are called to return the gift with our commitments. Jung (1938/54, p. 95-96; 1961/67, p. 284) describes human consciousness as a capacity to bring the world into being as sacred presence. This is the heart of the individuation process, and is as much about the presencing of the living world as about us as persons (Brooke, 1991).

The experience of that night has remained as a continuing background play of active imagination over the years. I did feel honored, and felt stirring the deep river of our common humanity and shared African landscape. On the other hand, I also have to acknowledge that my experience in iMfolozi comes back to me always with a sense of nostalgia and longing. The experience of the world's primal presence in that place is so powerful partly because it is marked off from the profane world of everyday life as a sacred space and a place of homecoming. It marks, therefore, its relative absence in our everyday lives, so that this play of presence (then) and reverie (now) is threaded with this nostalgic mood. As Romanyshyn (2002) says, "The paradox of reverie, its bittersweet quality of melancholy, is that it takes me home by awakening me to my sense of

74

homelessness" (p. 134).

This play of homecoming and homelessness may be the burden of being human, but perhaps not. The native Americans, for instance, were deeply at home in the world, nourished and held by the maternal earth. They were bewildered by the Europeans, who had little or no sense of their sacred and ecological place in a landscape that was alien to them, and which the Puritans regarded as the devil's domain (Romanyshyn, 1987). At least it can be said that the paradox of homecoming and homelessness is painfully sharpened with our western metaphysics and in our technological age (Mugerauer, 2008; Romanyshyn, 1989).

The village celebrations which came to me that night gather a certain kind of presence, which also tends to be rather lost into latency in our individualistic, productive, capitalist lives. The village celebrations remind one of a social, communal sensibility in which the community is not, as Jung tended to think, a threat to individual consciousness and the individuation process (Brooke, 2008). It is, rather, a sense of one's place in the social world, in which the personal is gathered and nurtured in a communal network of personal relations. We in the west typically think of humanist ethics as emerging out of the Judeo-Christian tradition and strengthening during the Enlightenment. However, there is an African humanism that has its own indigenous roots (Coetzee and Roux, 1998; Shutte, 1993). It is a humanism in which the fundamental structure and meaning of being human and ethics are understood as mutually implicated. There is a Zulu proverb which says, "*Umuntu ngumuntu ngabuntu.*"[3] Translated: "A person is a person through other persons." It is a position that is at the heart of the notion of *ubuntu*, which is the sense of community and ethical embeddedness intrinsic to the development of one's own humanity. We become fully human and find ourselves as persons only to the extent that we live with a sense of ethical responsibility towards an expanding community of others, both living and dead, and to the wider world at large. Being human is both a given and a task, and *ubuntu* is thus both given with the structure of being human and a spiritual calling for personal and ethical maturity.

To be welcomed into that village of warriors and their families, who had beaten off and then been conquered by the invading colonial army a hundred years earlier, was an extraordinary gift. It remains, for me, a guiding image of being human and the possibility of homecoming.

---

[3] All the "u" sounds are pronounced with a short, clipped "oo" as in "look."

References

Abram, D. (1996). *The spell of the sensuous*. New York: Vintage Books.

Abram, D. (2010). *Becoming animal*. New York: Pantheon Books.

Brooke, R. (1991). *Jung and phenomenology*. London and New York: Routledge. Also published in Pittsburgh: Trivium Publications, 2010.

Brooke, R. (2008). *Ubuntu* and the individuation process. *Psychological Perspectives*, 51, 36-53.

Coetzee, P. and Roux, A. (Eds.). *The African philosophy reader*. New York: Routledge.

Jung, C. (1938/54). Psychological aspects of the mother archetype. In *The Collected Works of C.G. Jung, Vol. 9.i., pp.* 73-110 Trans. R. Hull. Edited by Sir Herbert Read, M. Fordham, G. Adler; executive editor, W. McGuire. Bollingen Series XX, 20 volumes. London: Routledge; Princeton: Princeton University Press, 1953-1979.

Jung, C. (1952c). Synchronicity: an acausal connection principle. *Collected Works, Vol. 8*, pp. 417-519.

Jung, C. (1961/67). *Memories, dreams, reflections*. Recorded and edited by A. Jaffe. Trans. R. and C. Winston. The Fontana Library of Theology and Philosophy.

Mugerauer, R. (2008). *Heidegger and homecoming: The lietmotif in the later writings*. Toronto: University of Toronto Press.

Romanyshyn, R. (1987). Depression and the American dream: the struggle with home. In D. Levin (Ed.). *Pathologies of the modern self*. New York: New York University Press.

Romanyshyn, R. (1989). *Technology as symptom and dream*. London: Routledge.

Romanyshyn, R. (2002). *Ways of the heart: essays toward and imaginal psychology*. Pittsburgh: Trivium Publications.

Shutte, A. (1993). *Philosophy for Africa*. Marquette University Press.

Epiphanies of the Subtle World and a New Worldview in Jung's Psychology[1]

Veronica Goodchild

Christine de Pizan and the City of Ladies

Once upon a time in 1405 a gifted and highly respected mediaeval poet and writer, a woman of great talent and fortitude, Christine de Pizan by name, born in Italy but who lived in France, wrote a hauntingly inspirational book called *The Book of the City of Ladies*. According to her own biographical account, Christine, in a moment of dark despair about being a woman in a misogynist age, was visited in a waking vision by three majestic and noble women, of great beauty and wise demeanor, from another mysterious realm. These women informed her that because of her deep desire to acquire true knowledge, she had been chosen by God to construct a city with their help and their guidance. This place was called "the City of Ladies."

The construction of this city was to begin with Christine writing a book in which she would refute the derogatory accusations against women and confirm their strengths and gifts, by telling stories of heroines from the past and the present, tales of women who had distinguished themselves as poets, mystics, and royalty, as politicians, pirates, and warriors, as artists, teachers, and mothers, and as lovers and healers. Throughout these stories the virtues of women's compassion and constancy, fierceness and creativity, ingenuity and innate intelligence, and perhaps above all, love, shine through. Christine's book, written six hundred years ago, remains an inspired and inspiring gem, not only for women but also for the importance and validity of visionary knowledge. Christine was told that her City of Ladies would continue to be built and would be made with strong foundations and that its great walls, lovely moats, and lofty towers, would remain indestructible for all time.

Towards a New Worldview

But the moment when physics touches on the 'untrodden, untreadable regions,' and when psychology has at the same time

---

[1] A version of this paper was first given as a lecture at the International Association of Jungian Studies Conference in London, July 2006.

to admit that there are other forms of psychic life besides the acquisitions of personal consciousness...then the intermediate realm of subtle bodies comes to life again, and the physical and the psychic are once more blended in an indissoluble unity.... We have come very near to this turning point today. (C. G. Jung, Psychology and Alchemy, CW 12, par. 394)

The Age of Aquarius will involve the true discovery of the Divine Guest within us, and with it the need to recognize this in all people and in nature as well; it will be the dialectic of the individual and the cosmos...a deep understanding of the interdependence of all life...the unus mundus of the mystics and alchemists... the reemergence of Hagia Sophia, the feminine wisdom hidden in nature and in us. (Alice Howell, Jungian Synchronicity in Astrological Signs and Ages, pp. 207-209)

Of course we do not know if Jung ever read or even heard of Christine de Pizan, but that is not the point. Rather, the point is that visionary knowledge and this visionary way of knowing continues in Jung's work.

We've had a hundred years of non-locality and synchronicity, but depth psychologists lag behind quantum physicists in descriptions of a new worldview, which, however, are everywhere described, hinted at, and concealed in Jung's writings. The new co-ordinates of reality in both physics and psychology include: the chiasm of psyche and matter, the dissolution of ordinary time and space boundaries, the participation of the individual through the power of the *imaginatio vera* to co-create reality, the movement toward the *kairos* or present moment, and the breakthrough of eros awareness as a foundation for this new worldview. As an image of the soul, the City of Ladies is a bequest, a heritage, which in Jung's work is taken up again as a destiny. Do we not have an ethical obligation to follow soul into a new worldview, to consider seriously the implications of the epiphanies of this new worldview for the practice of our art, for reimagining the nature of experience, and for rethinking the language of our psychological traditions?

In my (2006) article in *Spring*, titled "Psychoid, psychophysical, p-subtle: Alchemy and a new worldview," and in my (2012) new book, *Songlines of the Soul: Pathways to a New Vision for a New Century*, I have described in detail how the many epiphanies of this new worldview, epiphanies of a subtle world, are manifested in experiences like synchronicities, UFOs, NDEs, crop circles, mystical cities. In addition, I have shown how these epiphanies of the subtle world, as anticipated and described in Jung's work on alchemy and the *imaginatio vera* as the true imagination, on synchronicities and UFOs, on the psychoid nature of the archetype, and his accounts of his own visionary experiences, from his encounters with Philemon, to his Ravenna vision and vision of the gold-green 'alchemical' Christ, have opened his psychology to these epiphanies of the subtle world as an Other world, and not just an underworld. In many respects, each of these themes in Jung's psychology is the construction of a new city of the soul, which takes his psychology beyond a psychology of the image, and into a psychology of encounter. It is sad to say, however, that the Jungian tradition, with few exceptions—Roderick Main, Remo Roth, and Jeff Raff—does not, as James Hillman once said to me directly, "go there." *Tant pis* for them, because the new worldview will break through whether we will it or not, just as Jung knew when he carved in stone above his house, "called or not, the gods will be present."

In this paper, I must for the sake of space considerations, limit myself to one example of how Jung's work is attuned to the subtle world.

Flying Saucers as Synchronicities on a Collective Scale

UFOs are a manifestation of a unified worldview, which Jung investigated as an epiphany of the subtle world. In his (1958) essay, "Flying Saucers, A Modern Myth," Jung noted that if these manifestations were both expressions of an archetypal compensation AND physically real, they would be examples of synchronicities on a collective level. The key point to note here is that, like synchronicities, UFOs would be a manifestation of the background *unus mundus* world. In his work with Wolfgang Pauli, Pauli described this background world as a psychophysical reality which consciousness differentiates as psyche and matter. For Jung, his studies of UFOs were on a continuum with his studies of alchemy. In his alchemical studies, Jung was progressively led away from the notion that the alchemists' visions were a projection of an interior psychic reality. Rather, as he noted in a passage in *Psychology and Alchemy* (CW 12), the alchemist did not think in either or terms. For Jung, therefore, the alchemists' visions were a radical re-imagining of the dichotomy of an inside, psychic space, and an outside, material world. These visions were manifestations of the *unus mundus* world, that background world where psyche is matter and matter is psyche. These alchemical studies and their contemporary expression in synchronicities and UFOS, are what led Jung to a radical re-visioning of the archetype as a psychoid realm. As a psychoid reality, the archetype belongs as much to nature as it does to psyche. The psychoid archetype dissolves the split between psyche and matter. The psychoid archetype is an archetype reconfigured for a *unus mundus* world.

In addition, I must point out, even if only in passing, that Jung's studies in alchemy emphasized the importance of the *imaginatio vera* as the "most important key to alchemy." The true imagination is, for Jung, a psychological force which co-constitutes and co-creates matter in its subtle form. True imagination was, for Jung, a real power to create images that are subtly corporeal, that are not fantasies, and that are more than mere unsubstantial thoughts. The *imaginatio vera* is the way in which we continue the work of creation. It is important to note here that without the true imagination, this subtle world remains only an abstract idea. The true imagination is the condition for the experience of the subtle world. One does not open to these realms by force or through reason alone. *Imaginatio vera* is the way of knowing that is also a way of being.

Although UFOs are synchronicities on a collective scale, there is a key difference between these two manifestations of the subtle world as a new worldview. Although both of them point to a unified worldview, the phenomenon of UFOs extends the reach of the subtle world. With synchronicities, the experience of the unification of psyche and matter in a meaningful way, points to the *unus mundus* world. With UFOs the experience of the unity of psyche and matter, points to the *unus mundus* as a *mundus imaginalis*, an imaginal world that is as real as our empirical world, but neither a world of perceptual facts nor conceptual ideas. Henri Corbin, the great interpreter of the Sufi mystics' exploration of this imaginal world coined the term imaginal in order to differentiate this world as a true world that is neither a psychological fantasy nor a factual material event. For Corbin, the perception of this real imaginal world, this third world that functions as a pivot for the material and mental worlds, requires a *cardiognosis*, a knowing through the heart, characterized by compassion, sympathy and love, an Eros way of knowing, rather than a logos centered knowing, an Eros gnosis figured as Sophia or Fatima. Corbin's cardiognosis is, I would claim, the true imagination. *Is it possible that it is this eros consciousness that draws UFOs into our experience?* A fact-minded literalism or a rational mode of knowing will simply not prepare us for this encounter. Do you think, for example, that the magnificent angels of mediaeval landscapes were matters of fact or reason? Eros consciousness was necessary then and as Romanyshyn (1989, 2002) has dramatically shown, angels began to disappear precisely at that moment when we began to take the world's measure. UFOs are perhaps angels in modern dress for those who have an open heart. The woodcut in Jung's essay on Flying Saucers, the "Spiritual Pilgrim Discovering Another World," makes it quite clear that the eruption of the *unus mundus / mundus imaginalis* into this world, is a matter of the heart (Romanyshyn, 2002, pp. 173-176). The epiphany of the *unus mundus / mundus imaginalis* into this world temporarily takes us out of linear history and exposes the seam of the time-bound to be also a timeless reality that opens our heart to the numinous. The experience of these eruptions is often felt as a deepening into a mystery. The local atmosphere ripples around us and quite often we have the sense of thoughts we did not know we had access to from a source of knowledge beyond ourselves. This is precisely how Jung, in his (1961) *Memories, Dreams, Reflections*, described his Ravenna vision or his alchemical vision of the green-gold Christ. We are often struck dumb in the sense that our ordinary and familiar language no longer suffices to describe these epiphanies of the subtle world, as we are drawn to a poetic sensibility in the effort to capture the subtle interplay of the timeless and the time-bound, the invisible and the visible. It is no wonder, therefore, that the literary critic Harold Bloom, in his splendid preface to Corbin's (1997) work on the Imaginal, cites the poet and the artist as contemporary exemplars of the Sufi mystics of long ago. The imaginal, Bloom notes, sometimes goes by no other name, than poetry itself.

Closing Reflections

But the depth psychologist is not a poet, and Jung has made it quite clear, that these epiphanies point in the direction of a new myth constellating in our time, due to changes in psychic dominants that accompany the move from Pisces to Aquarius, and he urges us to contemplate the psychic consequences of this astrological change.

In closing these remarks, I want to cite just a few examples of what we are called to contemplate.

First, UFO encounters and other manifestations of the subtle world, like NDEs, OBEs, ADEs, and Crop Circles, and other anomalous experiences, do challenge us to heal the split between a psyche that is inside and that has nothing to do with the world, and the physical world that is inanimate, without soul. Such dichotomous thinking has led to that "inconvenient truth" that the film of that name has so wonderfully demonstrated.

Second, the UFO encounters of the subtle imaginal world of the *mundus imaginalis* challenge us to adopt a new understanding of how the imaginal world is a new outside that is a spiritual landscape where beings have extension and dimension but of an immaterial kind. Corbin calls this new outside the Eighth Climate, and in this subtle place, we are being challenged into not only a new understanding of matter but also a new understanding of spirit. We are sojourners in this world in which we feel alive and awake, a stranger in a strange land. The journey to this Eighth Climate challenges us to get beyond our linear conceptions of time. In these epiphanies of the subtle imaginal world, we know we have been elsewhere, but we cannot describe the way to anyone else. Its geography is not a place on a map. These landscapes are the mystical cities of the soul, of which Christine de Pizan's *City of Ladies* was a beautiful expression six hundred years ago. In the spiritual literature of many cultures they have had numerous names, like Hurqalya, Shambhala, Avalon, and Olmo Lungring.

In truth, we live there by our birthright, and are only robbed of it, when we fall into time and we forget whence we have come.

Third, these epiphanies challenge us to prepare ourselves for encounters with the immortal guides of the soul, and to value the instantaneous and telepathic forms of communication, which J. B. Rhine's early experiments on parapsychological phenomena attempted to demonstrate. We dismiss these possibilities as irrational at our own peril, as if linear rational thinking were the only model of knowing. In addition we are challenged by these encounters with the immortal guides of the soul to a deeper sense of vocation that is devoted to the harmony of the whole of which we are a part. Such an awareness is the foundation for any true ecology that would heal our broken connection with nature.

The openness of Jung's psychology to the subtle realities of the *unus mundus / mundus imaginalis* posed far-reaching changes for consciousness, based on the establishment of the wisdom of compassion. The extraordinary manifestations of this subtle world that are and have been erupting, are attempts toward a new worldview in which the perishable is transformed into the imperishable. We stand on a threshold on one side of which is the potential for mass destruction, and on the other side of which is this seeming impossibility of a new breakthrough, which is the work of the new millennium.

References

Corbin, H. (1997). *Alone with the alone: Creative imagination in the Sufism of Ibn Arabi.* Princeton: Princeton University Press. Preface by Harold Bloom.
Jung, C. G. (1961). *Memories, dreams, reflections.* New York: Vintage.
Romanyshyn, R. D. (1989). *Technology as symptom and dream.* London and New York: Routledge.
Romanyshyn, R. D. (2002). *Ways of the heart: Essays toward an imaginal psychology.* Pittsburgh, PA: Trivium Publications.

Zombies as Abandoned Bodies

Robert Kugelmann

In *Technology as Symptom and Dream* (1989), Robert Romanyshyn explored the myths of modern technology. Significant in this account was discussion of "the abandoned body," by which he meant the envisioning of body devoid of subjectivity, the anatomical corpse that came into being in the symbolic year 1543, with the publication of Vesalius' treatise, *De humani corporis fabrica*. To conceive of the human body as *a* body rather than *some*body was a remarkable achievement, opening up the possibility for the natural scientific study of the flesh, resulting in the powers of contemporary medicine to do unprecedented things in times of illness and injury. The images of the abandoned body have been important for my own investigations of stress, pain, health, and irritable heart in the American Civil War. I was reminded of Romanyshyn's contribution to an understanding of the flesh in the modern world by the publication of *The Anticipatory Corpse* (2011) by Jeffrey Bishop. Drawing to a significant extant on other intellectual traditions, Bishop arrives at a similar insight into the image of the body that underlies medicine, especially when dealing with end-of-life issues, such as brain death and organ donation. For Bishop as for Romanyshyn, death is the *a priori* of the medical gaze into the body. We have an exceedingly difficult time seeing the boundaries between the living and the dead. The shadow of medical power has been a gnawing sense that our techniques govern us, rather than we them.

The desire to abandon the body has had a series of forms since the sixteenth century, and Romanyshyn saw the figure of the Astronaut as the most recent image of a desire to escape the flesh. The shadow of this desire, the abandoned body itself, has likewise had a number of forms, from the Witch of the Renaissance to the Hysteric and the Anorexic of the twentieth century. The shadow of the modern desire for transcendence of the terrestrial is the repressed flesh, always clamoring for return to us, because the truth of the matter is that we cannot abandon our bodies: We are neither angels nor devils, neither gods nor ethereal extra-terrestrials. While there are hopeful signs that some of us can learn to listen to flesh, return to earth, and descend into the flesh like the souls in Platonic philosophy, it does seem, as Bishop's book gives witness, that the polarity of the abandoned body and its shadow haunts us still.

If anything, it looks worse today than ever before. The polarity is taking on apocalyptic form. To be sure, nothing fires the western imagination better than the threat and the promise of the end of the world, and the popular fascination with The End remains strong. It has deep roots in our culture, to be sure, and it thrills and terrifies us. Thrills us: When I listen to some Christians telling me that We Are in the Last Days, it occurs to me that I wish we were. Then, I could relax and not be angst-filled with the mounting difficulties facing us, our children, and grandchildren in the twenty-first century. Of course, I am in the last days of my own life, even if the Grim Reaper has not indicated his arrival. Given the temporal structure of existence, moreover, we are always in the Last Days; it is a profound myth. If I were a theologian, however, I would say that we have too much work to do, and we will not get off the hook of our responsibilities as easily as a soon-to-be announced Second Coming of the Lord. Terrifies us: This may not be the best of all possible worlds, but it is not too bad. It is the only one we know, and to have all the beauty and sublime splendor of the cosmos destroyed raises the anxiety of annihilation. The apocalyptic imagination, however, is another thing. The abandoned body and its shadow have gotten sucked into the myth of the end.

Especially given the sad state of manned space flight in the United States at the current moment, to speak of the Astronaut as the vehicle for our escape from death and the flesh seems almost nostalgic. Space travel has become more down to earth, so to speak, and we know it means being cramped up in a small space with limited cuisine for an extended period. Elton John's song, "Rocket Man," captures something of the wistfulness of the Astronaut. No, the desire for transcendence of flesh and earth has mutated again. Now it appears in the form of the Singularity.

Verner Vinge (1993) called attention to what he called "Singularity," which he depicted in these terms: "The acceleration of technological progress has been the central feature of this century.... We are on the edge of change comparable to the rise of human life on Earth. The precise cause of this change is the imminent creation by technology of entities with greater than human intelligence." For Vinge, a mathematician and science fiction author, "superhumanity is the essence of the Singularity." Vinge does not celebrate the potentially looming arrival of a Post-Human epoch, and he considers the possibility that it will not happen. One of the possible ways it might, given the difficulties involved in Artificial Intelligence (AI), is the cultivation of Intelligence Amplification (IA), the teaming up of biological and technological devices of increasing sophistication: "Instead of simply trying to model and understand biological life with computers, research could be directed toward the creation of composite systems that rely on biological life for guidance or for the providing features we don't understand well enough yet to implement in hardware." These possibilities, some threatening the doom of humanity as it becomes redundant, others promising liberation from paralysis, blindness, and other limitations that come with the flesh, including death itself, are projected on to the near future. The Singularity takes us to where not even the Astronaut has trodden, although ease of space travel might be one of the consequences of the Singularity.

The dream of a flight from the human condition is still very much with us. Even if, through IA, humans, some at least, become quasi-immortal and interconnected with other post-humans and machines, will they think, feel, and will as we do? Vinge doubts it. So not only is flesh abandoned, so is mind and perhaps soul. Apocalyptic fantasies aside, what is striking about the Singularity is its collective character. It is not a new race of intelligent beings generating themselves on the horizon in this image with archetypal resonance for the current day; it is a suburban sprawl of fleshless nodes of instrumental reason. It presents an image of the Divine as omnipresent, omniscient, and eternal.

The Singularity is hardly masculine, or at best only vestigially so. Its erotic sense will be severely limited, because the Singularity presupposes something like the internet connecting the various nodes already. It would not be an individuated being; there would be no alienation because there would be no otherness.

The shadow of this aspiration to abandon the body has lost something of its femininity, just as Singularity is less masculine than the Astronaut. Romanyshyn saw the feminine in the shadow; it seems to be becoming genderless. The Anorexic was hungry, consuming metaphorically her own flesh, even as she symbolized the suffering of our repression of the flesh. The new shadow hungers after us, especially our brains. Zombies now figure the return of the abandoned body.

Zombies as they initially entered popular culture owed more to spiritualism and hypnotism, even though the earlier images of the Zombie lacked anthropological precision. The Zombie was in the control of someone else, a magician or a healer or an evil genius. Not so the new breed of Zombies, whose beginning may date from the 1985 movie, *The Return of the Living Dead*. The new breed of Zombies has common features. First, they seem to be the result of some technological innovation gone awry, or of some infection, some disease, that modern medicine cannot control. In any case, the Zombies have escaped technological control. Fears of worldwide epidemics, such as AIDS, SARS, and bird flu, are no doubt inspirational for the imagining of Zombies. Second, they are a mass phenomenon. They shuffle along in great hordes; there is nothing individuated about them, so that they reflect something collective about our culture. Third, they want us! They are oral beings, wanting communion with we the living. Fourth, this new breed eats brains.

Why brains? Just as brains figure in fantasies of the Singularity, with ours being only a template upon which new and improved computing systems can be built, so too with Zombies are brains the target. Before developing this theme, however, we must first anatomize Zombies. Zombies are rotting flesh, automatons who mindlessly hunt. They can be killed, so they must be alive, but they are more dead than alive. They apparently do not die on their own; they must be killed. As far as I know—but I am not an authority on them—there are no zombie dogs or cats. Just as in Cormac McCarthy's *The Road*, there are only the flesh-eaters and their prey, the remnants of humanity; animal life does not factor into the picture at all. In some depictions, Zombies have flesh hanging off their bones, resembling some of the images from Vesalius' great book. And as in Vesalius, the living cadavers assume poses of the living.

Just now, I called Zombies "living cadavers." I borrow this term from Bishop's *The Anticipatory Corpse*, where it signifies the status of the entity that is legally available for having its organ harvested, the term itself dating from the 1960s and the defining of brain death. The living cadaver arose because of "the structures . . . that define death lead to practices where the 'dead' are kept 'alive,' but the 'life' of the 'dead' is made possible only through the deployment of mechanical 'life' support" (p. 181). This condition, making actual Ivan Illich's proposal that we are entering an amortal society, has an ironic twist. With all due respect to those whose lives have been saved through organ donation, it is a fact that the living live because of what is harvested from these living cadavers. Dead persons; living cadavers.

Brain death "does not appear in print until 1968" (Bishop, p. 144) and the term was developed in order to facilitate organ donation (Bishop, p. 159). The category of brain death creates a paradoxical perceptual experience, of someone who appears alive, since the chest rises and falls in respiration, whose heart beats, but who is officially dead. This is the context in which the collective figure of the Zombies has emerged in the contemporary psyche. Zombies are brain dead, brain-devouring automatons.

They shadow the Singularity. Unlike the Vampire, their cultural rival in many ways, Zombies inspire no sympathy. Vampires are aristocrats, blood-addicts, often showing sophistication and savoir-faire. They are cruel, yet in the right circumstances, they can be charming. (At least this is true in the more contemporary versions of them.) The Vampire personifies the results of stress management, since they are strong and calm, with good coping skills. Zombies have nothing to do with stress. If Zombies show any emotion at all, it is anger or rage. In this rage, they attack.

What do Zombies want? In eating brains, they incorporate what they most vitally need, the source of consciousness and our humanity. The brain is the center of contemporary fascination, with research detailing hitherto unknown features and functions. The Decade of the Brain (1990-2000) followed on the heels of the rise of contemporary brain-eating Zombie. The brain, seat and source of consciousness, is the contemporary locus of almost everything having to do with the psyche. Zombies sense this, and they want to incorporate it. The attack of the Zombies marks an attempt to connect the flesh with the intellect. They may save us from the Singularity.

Often, Zombies haunt post-apocalyptic landscapes. What is going on here? Zombies inhabit the end of our time, the end of the modern epoch. Whether they signify something slouching toward Bethlehem, the consequences of our abandoning our bodies for too long, I suspect that they are more than shadows of our hubris. As in William Blake's "Marriage of Heaven and Hell," what appears evil does so only from our looking with distorted vision. Zombies have archetypal significance, to be sure; that significance includes the persistence of the body in the face of our angelic fantasies. The Zombie shuffle is a latter-day Dance of Death, urging us not to be so infatuated with our brains. The enhancement of the brain leads to the Singularity, a longing for immortality that will surely destroy us. The Zombie ties us to the earth, to the grave, to what St. Francis sang in "The Canticle of the Sun":

> Praised be You, my Lord,
> through our Sister Bodily Death,
> from whom no living man can escape.

Without that embrace, we are disembodied brains, or brain-dead.

90

References

Bishop, J. P. (2011). *The anticipatory corpse: Medicine, power, and the care of the dying.* University of Notre Dame Press.

Romanyshyn, R. D. (1989). *Technology as symptom and dream.* New York: Routledge.

Vinge, V. (1993). *The coming technological singularity: How to survive in the post-human era.* Available: http://www-rohan.sdsu.edu/faculty/vinge/misc/singularity.html

Abraxas and the Alchemy of Ice

Stanton Marlan

Over the years, I have considered Robert an important colleague and a good friend, one with whom I have always felt a deep resonance, both personally and in relation to our mutual interests in phenomenology and in Jungian and Archetypal psychologies. One particular place of this resonance has been a draw to the polar regions of psyche, to the paradoxes and "the issues that emerge when the human mind contends with the abyss beyond mental mapping" (Romanyshyn, 2008, p. 97). For me, the draw has been to alchemy's sol niger and, for Robert, the melting of polar ice, the theme of his remarkable essay entitled "The Melting Polar Ice: Revisiting Technology as Symptom and Dream." In both cases, the ego finds impasse, limits and, at times, defeat.

For Robert, the defeat of the ego is also seen as a defeat of "the despotic eye" and "the Spectator Mind" with their immovable beliefs, fixed gaze, and maintenance of power and control. The defeat of the ego can be a fearsome moment in psychic life that threatens rationality, our world view, and our vision of reality. In our own ways, I believe both Robert and I have attempted to stay with and engage such moments of defeat and to allow ourselves to be pulled by what he has passionately called an "erotic gravity" (Romanyshyn, 2008, p. 98) with a desire to both let go and respond to the nothing that turns out to be more than an abstract emptiness. As Jung has classically put it, a defeat for the ego is a victory for the Self. For Robert, the temptation to fall into the abyss is also a release into the imaginal where he engages the unfinished business of the soul. I believe this is the business of individuation, but as well the discovery of an oddity and a fundamental paradox of psychic life—namely, that the dissolution and darkness of defeat is at the same time a ground of illumination and a pathway to the numinous aspects of the soul's psychic life. It is a place of as yet unresolved and perhaps unresolvable mystery and at the edge of reason as we know it. Robert quotes Susan Rowland as stating, "Anything derived merely from rationality risks being profoundly inauthentic unless it also bears witness to the destabilizing influence of the unconscious" (as cited in Romanyshyn, 2008, p. 96).

For Robert, the edge of reason is also the edge of the Spectator Mind, surrounded in darkness. It is the place of *sol niger* and polar ice and the paradox of extremities. The radical coldness of the unconscious is relegated by James Hillman to the underworld, and he differentiates the hero's night sea journey from the *nekyia*, a descent "to a zone of utter coldness" (Hillman, 1979a, p. 168). For the hero there is a return from the journey, leaving the explorer "in better shape for the tasks of life," but from the *nekyia* there is no return. It is a journey to the underworld likened to Dante's Ninth Circle of *The Inferno*, a "frozen *topos*," "deep, deep down …. that is all ice."

> Here we are numb, chilled. All our reactions are in cold storage. This is a psychic place of dread and of a terror so deep that it comes in uncanny experiences, such as voodoo death and the *totstell* reflex. A killer lives in the ice. (Hillman, 1979a, p. 169)

For Hillman, the "glacial cold" (Hillman, 1979a, p. 169) of the underworld is likened to psychopathy, to figures such as Cain, Judas, and Lucifer, to the unredeemable, and yet such a place and such figures "serve a function in the soul," but for Hillman they cannot be reached by any religious or psychological humanism. For Hillman, the icy coldness of the underworld is "beyond human warmth" and must be met homeopathically in kind. In the clinical realm, the warm-hearted desire to show sensitive feelings to a paranoid or borderline patient is like showing blood to a vampire or a shark; one will quickly be eaten alive. For Hillman, the urge to warm the cold and melt the ice "reflects the therapeutic effort that has not been able to meet the ice at its own level. The curative urge conceals the fear of the Ninth Circle, of going all the way down" (Hillman, 1979a, p. 170) where we meet figures such as "Cain, Judas, and Lucifer by being aware of our own desires to be false and to betray, to kill our brother and to kill ourselves" (Hillman, 1979a, p. 169). Hillman notes that there is a part of our soul "that would live forever cast out from both human and heavenly company," and contact with these feelings is essential for any therapist who would truly work as a depth psychologist.

If we take Hillman's idea of the difference between the night sea journey and the *nekyia* seriously, i.e., that it is only the hero who returns from the journey in better shape for the tasks of life, what conclusion can we draw from those who have had the capacity to face such cold-blooded figures within ourselves? Are we no better off for doing so as therapists and human beings? Are we not able to engage life in a fuller way by connecting to our own psychopathic depths?

I would claim that we are, and I take Hillman's division between the night sea journey and the *nekyia* to be a polemical strategy to reveal something about the profound depths of psychic life that ordinarily remains invisible or unconscious. His strategy is a one-way exploration, with "singleness of intent," "a vesperal, into the dark" (Hillman, 1979a, p. 1) as he calls it. It is a strategy used both in *The Dream and the Underworld* and in his essay "Peaks and Vales" (Hillman, 1979b, pp. 54-74) where he draws apart *puer* and psyche. Ultimately, however, this one-sidedness cannot hold and Hillman seeks accommodation in the *puer*-psyche marriage. I would suggest that while much has been gained and continues to be gained through Hillman's polemical style, I nevertheless believe some kind of accommodation is also necessary for the divide between the hero's night sea journey and the *nekyia*. Both journeys hold out potential not simply for ego development, but also for the going under of the ego and the relativization of the Spectator Mind and despotic eye.

I believe Robert seeks such accommodation. In response to such extremities, his genius and gift has been to turn to the metaphoric and imaginal as a way of seeing in the dark with a soft eye, less Cartesian and with feeling. He performs "linguistic alchemy" which he describes as the dissolution of apodictic "certitude of the 'is' in the possibilities of the 'is not' and to hold the tension between them, between "dogmatic arrogance" and "cynical despair" (Romanyshyn, 2008, p. 96). For Robert, a poetic sensibility reaches into the archetypal core of such tensions, and he subtlety holds differentiations that are always turning into frozen opposites. What seems clear to me is that those who venture into the frozen depths can develop, as Hillman notes, a "psychological eye that sees all things from below ... an eye that glitters with ... inhuman insight ..." (Hillman, 1979a, p. 170). Is this the eye that Coleridge places in the brow of the Ancient Mariner when he interrupts the wedding guest to tell the story of his adventure into the frozen depths of his soul? Is his move into the unconscious a night sea journey or a *nekyia* to the underworld or both? It is a journey he returns from with a story important for modern consciousness. The Mariner's story holds us fast by his "glittering eye" and "skinny hand" as he recounts the eerie tale of literature's great nightmare voyage (Coleridge, 1900/2012). It is a tale he is compelled to tell and one we are compelled to hear. It is one of the tales that Robert also tells to mirror our modern consciousness that is dangerously unconscious of our blindness and its effects on our world.

---

[1] The Literature Network, http://www.online-literature.com/coleridge/646 (accessed August 20, 2012). All of the following quotations from this poem are taken from this web site.

The Mariner's heart is oblivious to life. He breaks a sacred trust and kills an albatross for no apparent reason. The consequences of this act set the stage for the psychic fate of the Mariner's descent into the unconscious. The Mariner cries out:

> Water, water, every where
> Nor any drop to drink.
>
> The very deep did rot …
> ….
> … slimy things did crawl with legs
> Upon the slimy sea.
> ….
> Alone, alone, all, all alone,
> Alone on a wide wide sea!
> And never a saint took pity on
> My soul in agony.

So the Mariner describes his *nigredo* world of despair where everything around him becomes poisonous. It is not surprising one would wish to turn away. "Poison, poison, every where … Nor a drop to drink" might be the motto for those of us who cannot take in the cold drought of our deeds and desires. But the Mariner is fully immersed in poisonous waters where the moon began to rise casting an odd light and mysterious shadow over the ship. Rather than turning away from the slimy waters, the Mariner looks directly into them and observes the "water-snakes." This is the moment in the rhyme where Robert notes the redemptive moment of the poem (2008, p. 110). The water-snakes "moved in tracks of shining white" and then appear with "rich attire: Blue, glossy green, and velvet black." For me, this is an alchemical moment and of the life that surges in the midst of death and shows its colors: white, blue, green, and black. The snakes "coiled and swam" and then everywhere "a flash of golden fire." The appearance of golden fire has archetypal significance and in it death and illumination are closely linked in a mercurial tincture signifying that redemption is not something that leaves poisoned water behind but rather shines through them.

The Mariner's transformation would seem to result from an awareness of the unearthly light of the moon, which at the same time is a light of nature, a *lumen naturae*. It is an odd light that illuminates in the shadows, a glow of darkness in which a fuller effulgence of colors, like a peacock's tail, signals the emergence of Eros. In a golden flash, things have changed and the Mariner speaks to the snakes:

> O happy living things! no tongue
> Their beauty might declare:
> A spring of love gushed from my heart,
> And I blessed them unaware:
> ....
>
> The selfsame moment I could pray;
> And from my neck so free
> The Albatross fell off, and sank
> Like lead into the sea.

In this moment, the Mariner is able to feel gratitude for life itself in all its forms and his feeling life is unfrozen, there is a softening of his heart, and he is moved to the core of his being. The unfreezing of emotion is already the beginning of the redemption of the Mariner's "despotic eye," the eye that "never sheds a tear" (Romanyshyn, 2008, p. 108) never sees blue, begins to become conscious.

Continuing in this vein, Derrida has noted "only man knows how to go beyond seeing and knowing, because only he knows how to cry.... Only he knows that tears are the essence of the eye—and not sight." "Eyes that cry implore rather than see; they invite the question from the other: whence the pain?" (Derrida as cited in Jay 1994, p. 523). Such an eye moves beyond despotic sight and reveals a soulful awareness that glows with blueness, an eye of the heart unknowable to the Mariner until the moment of his redemption.

I would claim that the humanity of the Mariner's redemptive vision is not that of "tepid balance" or "Christianism's bleeding heart" (Hillman, 1979a, p. 169) that Hillman has taught us are not adequate to penetrate the underworld—and yet is a heart open to deep feeling. While such feeling is essential, it may not be enough. Robert has observed that the Mariner's redemption is short lived. He is in the end unable to hold the tension between the light of the sun and the darkness of the moon. He is unable to wed what is above and what is below. At the end of the Rime, the Mariner is drawn toward the conventional sentiments of traditional religion, the vespers of the church, and, for Robert insofar as the Mariner is an archetypal example for negotiating the depths, he "does not augur well for us who are [his] archetypal descendants" (Romanyshyn, 2008, p. 110). Traditional Christianity continues to split off the demonic coldness of the serpent, which according to Jung continues to fall into the shadow. For Romanyshyn, in order for the Mariner to achieve a deeper transformation, he "would have required that the Serpent be given its place on the cross alongside the Christ" (2008, p. 112).

Such a radical vision would seem to suggest that alongside the value of a compassionate heart, the cold, instinctual, and demonic energies of the soul must also be given their place as co-equal archetypal forces in our vision of our humanity. Beyond the idea of a warm heart and warm feelings are feelings of another sort. Redemption for the Mariner must not be an enantiodromia from unfeeling coldness to a warm and innocent heart. There is another kind of heart in the

> icy chasm of Christianism's shadow .... The heart has a coldness, a place of reserve ... that preserves, holds, protects, isolates, suspends animation and circulation, an alchemical congelation of substance. The cruelty and mean despising are the surroundings of a private sense of ultimate deepening. (Hillman, 1974a, pp. 169-170)

—side by side, the heart of Christ and the heart of Lucifer. How strange is the human soul! The heart is complex, needing to be capable of a wide range, full of love and compassion and yet cool as a serpent's eye. Strange bedfellows, to be sure, but such is the archetype of wholeness, a true *coniunctio oppositorum*. Though the imagery of Christ and the cross in Robert's vision utilizes Christian symbolism, the placement of the serpent on the cross strains the religious paradigm to a breaking point, to Gnostic blasphemy. Perhaps this is the step that Coleridge could not take in his life or Rime?

Perhaps this is the step that awaited the advent of Jung's depth psychology and his encounter with the terrible and dreadful Gnostic deity Abraxas, whom Shamdasani describes as "the uniting of the Christian God with Satan" (cited in Drob, 2012, p. 236). Robert's intuition about the importance of elevating the serpent to the cross and of a vision where coldness is brought to the level of divinity, in fact recalls Jung's notion of Abraxas. It is hard to come to terms with the implications of such a vision. Jung struggles to come to terms with this divinity in his *Red Book*.

There the dead "wish to know more about the 'highest God,' ... Abraxas. We are told that this God draws the *summum bonum* from the sun and the *infinum malum* from the devil. .... that Abraxas himself is *LIFE*, 'the mother of good and evil.'" (Jung cited in Drob, 2012, p. 236). He is "both the sun and 'the eternally sucking gorge of emptiness,' both life and death, 'truth and lying,' good and evil, light and darkness" (Jung cited in Drob, 2012, p. 236). In short, Jung calls Abraxas "terrible" and "a monster of the underworld" (cited in Drob, 2012, p. 236). Such a characterization for Sanford Drob "invokes comparison not only with the unconscious, but with the broad conception of the 'monstrous' [as] unforeseeable future" (2012, p. 236)). Like Derrida's notion of the monstrous (Jung, cited in Drob, 2012, p. 237), "Abraxas can be understood as the awesome future that can neither be anticipated nor circumscribed by words. Before him is no question and no reply" (Jung cited in Drob, 2012, p. 237). Abraxas is "'chaos,' the 'utterly boundless,' 'eternally incomprehensible ... cruel contradictoriness of nature.'" (Jung cited in Drob, 2012, p. 236). Abraxas, we are told, "is the world, its becoming and its passing" (Jung cited in Drob, 2012, p. 236). Perhaps such a deity stands behind the phenomena of both *sol niger* and the melting ice—so painful to look at and recognize!

For this reason, I am grateful to Robert Romanyshyn for his unflinching look into the darkest aspects of the Spectator Mind and despotic eye—into the deep shadows of modern consciousness and to what is frozen and split off in the depths of psyche, soul, and nature. He does not rush to save or redeem, but first to look, listen, and then respond to the appeal of the collective psyche, to go and sit in the cold and in so doing to hear the appeal of melting ice, an awakening call about the condition of our soul and planet. His eye does not blink, but his heart does not freeze. He trusts his feelings and awakens his feeling function, making a judgment about the appeal of nature and soul. His sense-itivity to the world and his symbolic attitude reads nature to find soul, to see the signs and symptoms that show themselves when one makes a place for the unconscious. In so doing, his work has a tale to tell and, like the Mariner's, I believe it is one we must hear.

References

Coleridge, S.T. (1900/2012). The rime of the ancient mariner. The Literature
    Network: http://www.online-literature.com/coleridge/646 (accessed

98

August 20, 2012).

Drob, S. (2012). *Reading the Red Book: An interpretive guide to C.G.
Jung's Liber Novus*. New Orleans: Spring Journal Books.

Hillman, J. (1979a). *The dream and the underworld*. New York: Harper
& Row.

Hillman, J. (1979b). Peaks and vales. In *Puer papers* (pp. 54-74). Irving,
TX: Spring Publications.

Jay, M. (1994). *Downcast eyes*. Berkeley: University of California Press.

Romanyshyn, D. (2008). The melting polar ice: Revisiting technology as
symptoma and dream, *Spring, 80*, 79-116.

Jung's Warning about Faith:
The Psychological Danger of Belief

David L. Miller

> And the desire to believe in a metaphor
> ... is to stick to the nicer knowledge of
> Belief, that what it believes in is not true.
>
> —Wallace Stevens (1975, p. 332)

Introduction: Belief Blitz

Like Robert Romanyshyn's book, *Mirror and Metaphor*, which refers centrally to two poems by Wallace Stevens (2001, p. 3, 181-183), this essay in Robert's honor has as its starting point lines from yet a third poem by Stevens. Robert's book had as its argument the notion that a cultural history of science, including particularly the science of psychology, is a history of metaphors. The language of science, Robert held, is not transparent to things. It is opaque, because it is fundamentally metaphoric. This idea calls into question the beliefs held by scientists, including psychologists, especially the beliefs that those holding them take to be true. It is the matter of belief that I wish to address as an addendum to Robert's argument.

That the matter of belief may be important is addressed by a warning of C. G. Jung, a warning that he may not always have himself heeded. In the early part of the 20th century, Jung wrote in the "Scrutinies"[1] section of *The Red Book*: "I believe [!] that it is better in our time if belief is weak.... It is dangerous to believe too much" (2009, pp. 335-336). As if echoing Jung a century later, there have recently appeared books from widely diverse perspectives that complain of the dangers of belief. To name

---

[1] "Scrutinites" is the English translation of Jung's term *Prüfungen*. This is somewhat misleading, if not inflationary, since the word in German means something like "tries," "trials," or "just testing," i.e. Jung was trying out some reflections to see how they seem. The passage, two paragraphs long in all, does not correspond to anything in the *Black Book*, which most of the so-called "Scrutinies" does, but it was presumably written near May of 1914 when Jung was 39. Compare the important Derridean reflections on the French equivalent of the German word *Prüfungen*, i.e., *épreuve*, in William Robert, *Trials of Antigone and Jesus*, pp. 2-4, and in fact the entire book and its argument about the notion of "trials."

only six of the most prominent of these, there are (in chronological order): Slavoj Žižek, "Faith without Belief," *On Belief* (2001); Daniel Noel, "The Belief Files—A Modern Myth in Media Culture," *In a Wayward Mood: Selected Writings, 1969-2002* (2004); Julia Kristeva, *This Incredible Need to Believe* (2006); James Carse, *The Religious Case against Belief* (2008); Harvey Cox, *The Future of Faith* (2009); and, Simon Critchley, *The Faith of the Faithless* (2011). As in Jung, there is in these books a blitzkrieg against what the authors take to be a cultural belief blitz in our time.

One surely can understand, after the terror of 9/11/2001, that belief can be dangerous to the health of the body politic. What I want to inquire into is why belief may also be dangerous psychologically.

I. Traduttore, traditore: To Translate is to Betray.

My concern about belief business began in 1957 in a Greek class. The professor had a pedagogical technique that involved sending the students to the blackboard. He would come round and write a Greek text in front of each student, which the student was then to translate. One day he wrote the following in front of me: "*ho pisteuō eis ton huion tou theou.*" I knew that the passage was from Christian scripture (I John 5.10). And I knew that the usual translation was "The one believing in the son of God …."

But there was a problem with this translation, or so I thought. The verb *pisteuein* is the same word as the noun *pistis*. That is, Greek does not have a doublet like English (noun "faith" and verb "belief"). So, literally the Greek verb should be translated "to faith." Also, Greek verbs take particular prepositions. The Greek *pisteuein* takes the preposition *eis*, which means "into."[2] Greek has a perfectly good word for "in," namely, *en*, but the Greek verb that is often translated "to believe" does not take "in." It takes "into." So, I wrote on the blackboard the following: "The one faithing into the son of God." This was greatly to the amusement of my fellow students, but it was not in the least amusing to the professor! But

---

[2] Arndt, William F. & F. Wilbur Gingrich. *A Greek-English Lexicon of the New Testament and Other Early Christian Literature*, pp. 665-670. See *Novum Testamentum Graece*, p. 236, where codices are identified that have different prrepositions that are sometimes used later with pisteuei'n [*pisteuein*].

if the Greek text does not mean "believe in" something, what, I wondered, could it mean?[3]

There is no problem in Latin. For example, the Vulgate of St. Jerome, a fifth century translation of the Greek New Testament that was commissioned by Pope Damasus I in 382 C.E., says clearly, *Qui credit in Filium Dei* ["The one who believes in the Son of God"]. Latin has no problem, because it, like English, has a doublet as between the noun (*fides* = "faith") and the verb (*credere* = to believe). But I wondered whether, when Christianity was translated into Latin from Greek, a fundamental meaning might have shifted, or even that an important meaning was forever lost that is not reflected, but masked, in the shift in language. My wonderment is similar to the observation by Martin Heidegger that the meaning of being shifted in the transition from Greek to Latin vernacular and syntax.[4]

I am not the only one to have felt uneasy about "belief" as opposed to faith. Theologians through the years have also worried when *fides* is taken to mean *assensus*. Melancthon and Luther for example, preferred the word *fiducia* to the word *fides*, because *fiducia* is less likely to be confused with belief *in* some-*thing* taken to be true. *Fiducia* means "trust" or "confidence" and is more like faith than it is like belief. And now in our time, along comes C. G. Jung, who seems also concerned about belief, but for psychological, and not theological, reasons.

II. Jung's Psychological Warning: Belief is Psychologically Dangerous

Jung's warning about the psychological danger of belief is not limited to *The Red Book.* In the foreward to Victor White's book, *God and the Unconscious,* Jung writes that when persons today get into a believing mode they place themselves in "medieval" times or psychologically "living in the year 5000 B.C." Believing makes them "troglodytes and barbarians" though they live in the 20th or 21st century (*CW,* 11 para., 463). And in a letter to Victor White, Jung says: "I can say my life-work is essentially an attempt to understand what others apparently can believe" (*Letters,* 1 para. 502). Again to Father White, when he was 70 years old Jung writes: "I began my career with repudiating everything that smelt of belief" (2007, p. 6). And to another theologian, Bernhard Martin, Jung is forceful : "I grant you that the believer will learn nothing from my *Answer to Job* since

---

[3] In the early seventies, in *Gods and Games: Toward a Theology of Play*, pp. 166-67, I wrote briefly about this problem of the Greek verb taking the preposition "into." But I did not go into the matter deeply in that book, and I have let the enigma rest for forty years until now.

[4] Martin Heidegger, *On Time and Being*, tr. J. Stambaugh (New York: Harper and Row, 1972), p. 7, compare pp. 9, 17, 66; Martin Heidegger, *The End of Philosophy*, tr. J. Stambaugh (New York: Harper and Row, 1973), p. 13, compare pp. 27, 28, 55

he already has everything. I write only for unbelievers. Thanks to your belief, you know much more than I do…. I am not concerned with what is 'believable' but simply with what is knowable…. l cannot anticipate a thing by believing it but must be content with my unbelief" (Letters, 2 para 197, 199).

Though Jung's language is strong, his reasoning is weak. Jung contrasts belief and knowledge in these quotations, and already in *The Red Book*, he likens believing to childhood (presumably both individual childhood and the childhood of the race) and knowledge to being grown up. The weakness in these binarisms is that they are not psychological, and they do not accord with Jung's own view of the psyche in which complexes are governed by the logic of synchronicity, not diachronicity. The child-belief and adult-knowledge dichotomy is not dialectical, but is dualistic. It is split-off thinking, and is characterized by a one-sided developmentalism. It does not sound like the Jung of the idea of the self as a *complexio oppositorum*, where presumably one is always both child and adult, both a believer and an unbeliever.

Jung comes closer to a compelling psychological logic for his worry about belief in at least three places where he speaks about the psychological intimacy of belief and doubt. In writing about the doctrine of the Trinity in Christianity, Jung says: "It is dangerous if these matters are only objects of belief, for where there is belief there is doubt [*Zweifel*] and the fiercer and naiver the belief the more devastating the doubt [*Gedanke*] once it begins to dawn" (*CW*, 11, para 294). Earlier in the same essay, Jung writes: "People who merely believe and don't think always forget that they continually expose themselves to their own worst enemy: doubt. Wherever belief reigns, doubt lurks in the background" (*CW*, 11, para 170). And in the Zarathustra seminar Jung is even stronger. He says:

> When somebody doubts the truth which you believe, he is an offender because he has given you a bad example; you are offended because instantly the doubt can spring up in yourself too. There is danger that you may doubt that which you believe; therefore, [there is an impulse in the history of religions to] kill those people who doubt [what you believe] and in this way you [believe that you can] remove doubt… And that is the psychology of those pious people who think it is terrible if one says there is no God or something of the sort, one should not say such things. One *ought* to believe something or want to believe something, I become exceedingly intolerant; I don't like anybody who reviles

my beloved ideas because I make such an effort to believe them. (1988, pp. 849-850)

Indeed, elsewhere in the Zarathustra seminar Jung twice makes a distinction between "belief" (German *Glauben*) and the word *pistis*, which he writes in Greek. He says that the latter does not mean "believe," but means "trust" (German *Vertrauen*) and "loyalty" (German *Loyalität*).[5] It almost seems as if Jung—perhaps intuitively or unconsciously—is trying to restore to the notion of "belief" the old Greek (pre-Latin) idea of "faith." Why? Because, as Jung says, "Belief … is your own activity," (1988, p. 294), i.e., it is a matter of "ego" and not the deep self. Indeed, Freud wrote in a letter of May 31, 1897: "Belief … is a phenomenon that belongs wholly to the system of the ego (the Conscious) and has no counterpart in the Unconscious." (1953, p. 255).[5]

This is why, in English, one cannot say "I faith," but one can say "I believe," because faith has nothing to do with ego whereas belief does. So, belonging to ego consciousness (an ego economy, an ego domain), belief splits off doubt, often projecting it on someone else, and then belief takes on the force of knowledge, of thinking it knows something. The point is that belief can cut off reflection and complex understanding. Belief believes. This is why it is psychologically dangerous. It reduces everything in a one-sided way to ego consciousness, and loses a depth of psyche. The reason that belief is dangerous is that it keeps one in the logic of the economy of the ego and is not psychological in the deepest sense.

"I" believe. The "I" believes. And therefore it cannot move into the larger economy of the self. Like hope, which can be a defense against grief,[6] belief is a defense mechanism, a defense against reflection and realistic understanding, a defense against making conscious psyche's logic, which is always two-sided and dialectical (remember that Jung defined neurosis as one-sidedness, nothing-but, *nicht als*). Belief represses reflection. I imagine that this is why Jacques Lacan said that "a Catholic [i.e., a believer] is unanalyzable" (*un catholique est inanalysable*) (1976, p. 9). It makes a person unanalyzable. It also may be why Kafka wrote: *Ein*

---

[5] C.G. Jung, Nietzsche's Zarathustra, pp. 909, 929-930; cf. C.G. Jung, Collected Works, 10.521; 11.167.

[6] See Martha Stark, "Transformation of Relentless Hope: A Relational Approach to Sadomasochism, http://www.lifespanlearn.org/documents/STARKtransform.pdf, accessed 10/4/10, and Jancy Van Dyke Platt, "What Will Happen to the Flowers When Winter Comes/" *Journal of Religion and Health*, 16/4 (1977): 326ff.

Glaube wie ein Fallbeil.... ("A belief is like a guillotine..."), (Kafka Project, n.d.), i.e., it cuts off the head, the reflection, it remains undialectically and unpsychologically one sided. It is fixated and it is dangerous to the health of the psyche. So Lacan said in an interview in Rome in 1974: "If religion triumphs, psychoanalysis fails (1975).[7]

Belief stops reflection because it thinks it knows something. Doubt becomes unconscious. It cannot see an-other, the other-ness. There cannot be a making conscious. And this is as true of the analyst and her or his believed-in theories as it is of the client and her or his believed-in neurotic complexes.

Conclusion: Faithing Into

So far so good, but the matter of a possible meaning of *pisteuō eis*, "faithing into," is still not clear. I actually never solved the problem of a possible mistake made in Christianity by the translation misunderstanding as one moves from Greek to Latin and then into English. I never solved it, but my daughter did, fifteen years after my embarrassment in the Greek class. One evening about thirty years ago, at a winter dinner table of our family in upstate New York, my daughter said abruptly, "Take me skiing tonight." It was snowing, the roads were slick, the temperature was well below freezing, and I was certain that the conditions on the ski slope were icy. So I protested. But she responded with a look that every father of a teenage daughter knows well, "Oh, Dad! I don't care if the evening is terrible, you know that I am so into skiing!" There it is in the contemporary street English of today's youth! and it is now also a part of the adult lexicon, too. The use of the preposition "into" seems to have reverted to an ancient meaning.

Being "into" skiing is not a matter of "believing" in skiing. Belief has nothing to do with it. My daughter's assent, or volitional trust, or personal confidence are not to the point. There is a huge difference between "believing in" something and "faithing into." "Faithing into" is a pact or commitment that does not insist on the personal assumption of a personal subject who is a believer. "Faithing" happens—some would say by grace—and then "I" am *into* it, into *it*, willy nilly, whether "I" will or no. "Faithing" is not produced or merited by my joining the Crusades or becoming a suicide bomber. "Believing in something" has nothing to do with "faithing into." My daughter does not have to believe in skiing—an

---

[7] Cf. James Hillman, On Paranoia (Dallas: Spring Publications, 1988), p. 39: "When Jacques Lacan warned...that psychoanalysis is over...should religion triumph, I understand him to mean, "Psychology is impossible wherever literaly meanings triumph."

absurd and nonsensical idea—in order to be "into" it. Skiing happened to her. It doesn't happen to everyone. Tennis happens to some. Or kayaking. Even religion.

But the religion that happens to some is not the same as belief in something and belief systems. I am not the only one to insist upon this. Jacques Derrida, for example, in a conversation at Villanova in 1994 put the matter clearly. He said:

> I would distinguish between religion and faith. If by religion you mean a set of beliefs, dogmas, or institutions—e.g., the church— then I would say that religion as such can be deconstructed, and not only can be but should be deconstructed, sometimes in the name of faith.... You cannot address the other, speak to the other, without an act of faith, without testimony. What are you doing when you attest to something? You address the other and say, "believe me." Even if you are lying, even in a perjury, you are addressing the other and asking the other to trust you. This "trust me, I am speaking to you" is of the order of faith, a faith that cannot be reduced to a theoretical statement, to a determinative judgment; it is the opening of the address to the other. So this faith is not religious, strictly speaking; at least it cannot be totally determined by a given religion. (1997, pp. 21f)

Slavoj Žižek, in an essay entitled "Faith without Belief," concurs:

> When I say 'I have faith in you,' I assert the symbolic pact between the two of us, a binding engagement, the dimension which is absent in simple 'believing in ...' Then he adds: "One can believe in ghosts without having faith in them. (2001, p. 109)

Harvey Cox, in a recent book entitled *The Future of Faith*, cites the provocative but telling mock prayer of Aldous Huxley: "Give us this day our daily faith, but deliver us from beliefs" (cited in 2009, p. 213).

These recent comments distinguishing belief from authentic faith recall to mind the poetic lines of Wallace Stevens, with which I began. And they bring to mind, also, other lines of Stevens with which I will end.

> The final belief is to believe in a fiction,
> which you know to be a fiction,

there being nothing else.

—Wallace Stevens (1977, p. 163)

References

Arndt, W.F. & Gingrich, F.W. (1957). *A Greek-English lexicon of the New Testament and other early Christian literature.* Chicago: University of Chicago Press.

Carse. J. (2008). *The religious case against belief.* New York: Penguin Books.

Cox, H. (2009). *The future of faith.* New York: HarperOne.

Critchley, S. (2011). *The faith of the faithless.* Cambridge: Harvard University Press.

Derrida, J. (1997). *Deconstruction in a nutshell.* (J. D. Caputo, Ed.). New York: Fordham University Press, 1997.

Freud, S. (1953). *Standard Edition.* (J. Strachey, Trans). London: Hogarth Press.

Heidegger , M. (1972). *On time and being.* (J. Stambaugh, Trans.). New York: Harper and Row.

Heidegger, M. (1973). *The end of philosophy.* (J. Stambaugh, Trans.). New York: Harper and Row.

Hillman, J. (1988). *On paranoia.* Dallas: Spring Publications.

Jung, C. G. (1973). *Letters.* (R. F. C. Hull, Trans.). Princeton: Princeton University Press,

Jung, C. G. (1988). *Nietzsche's Zarathustra.* (J. Jarrett, Ed.). Princeton: Princeton University Press.

Jung, C. G. (1953-1979). *The collected works.* (R. F. C. Hull, Trans.). Princeton: Princeton University Press.

Jung, C. G. (2009). *The red book: Liber Novus.* (S. Shamdasani, Ed.). New York: W. W. Norton & Company.

Jung, C. G. & White, V. (2007). *The Jung-White letters.* (A. C. Lammers & A. Cunningham, Trans.). London: Routledge.

Kafka, F. (n.d.). Aphorism #87. Retrieved from http://www.kafka.org/index/php?aphorisme.

Kristeva, J. (2006). *This incredible need to believe.* (B. B. Brahic, Trans.). New York: Columbia University Press.

Lacan, J. (1975). "Conferences de presse au Centre francais," Rome 10/29/1974. In *Letters de L'Evole freudienne de Paris, 16.*

Lacan, J. (1976). *Seminar of 16 March 1976,* p. 9. http://archive.nosubject.com/seminares/SeminaireXXIII/1976.03.16.pdf.

Miller, D. (1973). *Gods and games: Toward a theology of play.* New York: World Publishing Co.; New York: Harper Colophon Books.

Noel, D. (2004). The belief files—A modern myth in media culture. In E. Nestle (Ed.), *In a wayward mood: Selected writings, 1969-2002.* New York: iUniverse, 2004.

Robert, W. (2010). *Trials of Antigone and Jesus.* New York: Fordham University Press.

Romanyshyn, R. (2001). *Mirror and metaphor: Images and stories of psychological life.* Pittsburgh: Trivium Publications.

Stevens, W. (1975). *Collected poems.* New York: Alfred A. Knopf.

Stevens, W. (1977). *Opus posthumous.* New York: Alfred A. Knopf.

Žižek, S. (2001). *On belief.* New York: Routledge.

Romanyshyn and the Historical Retrieval of My Intellectual Heritage within an Existential Personalist Ethics

Brent Dean Robbins

While Robert Romanyshyn rightly identifies as a depth psychologist, his deep roots are within the tradition of existential phenomenology and – while, to some, this might be surprising – I would also situate Romanyshyn's work within a tradition of social ethics, existential personalism. These influences – existentialism, phenomenology and personalist ethics – are also at the very heart of humanistic psychology.

A Genealogy

When I was a visiting assistant professor at Allegheny College, I developed a friendship with one of my colleagues who taught a course on the history of psychology. An assignment in the class required the students to each choose a favorite instructor of psychology and to perform an academic geneaology. This geneaology involved a simple process of tracing the professor's dissertation. Once the dissertation chair is identified, the student goes on in turn to track down the chair of that person's dissertation, and so on. This task is repeated with each dissertation chair until the trail runs dry – as far back in history one can go.

I was flattered one semester when several students decided to trace my own intellectual heritage. As they discovered, I completed my doctoral dissertation under the direction of Michael Sipiora at Duquesne University. Michael, in turn, defended his own dissertation under the chairmanship of Robert Romanyshyn at University of Dallas. When the students traced the dissertation Chair of Romanyshyn, it took them right back to Duquesne University, where Romanyshyn's dissertation was chaired by the revered figure, Rolf von Eckartsberg. None of this was a surprise to me – these links were common knowledge.

What astonished me was the direction of the investigation from that point forward. Von Eckartsberg had earned his doctorate from the prestigious Harvard University, and I'd associated him with Timothy Leary and Richard Alpert (aka, Ram Dass). But more importantly, Von

Eckartsberg did his dissertation under the direction of Gordon Allport. This link to Allport is very significant because perhaps no single person had more influence on the emergence of the Third Force of humanistic psychology than Allport did (DeCarvalho, 1991).

Allport had been a student at Harvard and was closely associated with William James there. But in fact he completed his dissertation in Germany under the Chairmanship of Sidney Langfield, who in turn did his dissertation with Carl Stumpf. Stumpf was the main influence on Gestalt psychology and was also a primary influence on the early thinking of Edmund Husserl, the father of phenomenology. By following Stumpf's intellectual heritage, the students were led all the way back to Immanuel Kant and then to Leibniz.

This lineage makes for a beautiful symmetry, for a variety of reasons.

While Allport is famous primarily as a psychologist, his dissertation and his appointment at Harvard University was within the field of social ethics. I think this preoccupation with the intersection of psychology, phenomenology and ethics is the common ground that can be identified from Kant to little old me. My colleagues who studied with Michael Sipiora, such as Robert McInerney and Rex Olson, for example, have a similar preoccupation with social ethics, psychology, and critical continental philosophy, with an emphasis on phenomenology. These same preoccupations are found in the work of Romanyshyn.

At the time Gordon Allport was studying social ethics in Germany, the field of post-Kantian ethics was being profoundly influenced by students of Edmund Husserl, such as Dietrich von Hildebrand and Edith Stein. Max Scheler's (1973) existential phenomenology became a focal point of this emerging ethics which is most often identified under the category of existential personalism.

It was precisely this emerging conception of the person that deeply informed the work of Gordon Allport (Allport, 1937). From out of his studies of social ethics, Allport quite literally invented the sub-field of psychology that we now call personality theory – a field that simply did not exist until Allport breathed life into it – despite opposition at the time from the dominant academic worldview of behaviorism.

It was Allport's emphasis on the person as an ethical being (and the underlying philosophical anthropology of this mindset) that became the foundation of the Third Force, humanistic psychology (DeCarvalho, 1991) – which of course is also often referenced as person-centered theory, especially when identified with the theory and practice of Carl Rogers (1979).

Personalism and Humanistic Psychology

All of the major founders of humanistic psychology – Carl Rogers, Abraham Maslow, Rollo May, etc. – looked to their senior colleague Gordon Allport as the harbinger of a new and viable alternative to the reductionism represented by behaviorism and classical psychoanalysis. These forces of behaviorism, classical psychoanalysis and other forms of reductonism, such as psychophysiology, respectively dissolved the person into forces essentially devoid of the kind of dignity necessary to ground a viable and persuasive social ethics as it was coming into being at this point in history – giving life, for example, to the United Nations Universal Declaration of Human Rights – which was authored in part, for example, by Jacques Maritain, a major thinker within the tradition of existential social ethics, and co-drafted by Lebanese existential philosopher, and personalist, Charles Malik (Dougherty, 2003).

Humanistic psychology promised a new vision of psychology which, by saving the appearances, so to speak, through an existential and phenomenological approach, promised to revive the personalist foundation of contemporary social ethics.

The German social ethics of Max Scheler (1973), Edith Stein (1989) and Dietrich von Hildebrand (2009) had influences that were felt across Europe and America.

A Polish philosopher, Karol Wojtyla, was inspired to develop his own adumbration of a phenomenological personalist ethics (Woznicki, 1980), which culminated in hugely influential texts such as *Love and Responsiblity*. Wojtyla of course went on to become the famous figure of Pope John Paul II – appointed Pope largely due to the monumental influence Wojtyla had had in the development of documents associated with the Second Vatican Council – an event that "modernized" the Church in ways that were and still are earth-shattering – including the idea that anywhere Love and Truth is occurring in the universe – whether or not under the tutelage of the Papacy – there God and Christ come into Being. Taken seriously, a Buddhist can tap into Christ-consciousness as much as, say, a Capuchin Monk (see for example: Flader, May 6, 2012).

This Pope's influence could be felt in Catholic Universities across the pond here in the United States. Fordham University for example has been one of the few places where a phenomenological psychologist was able to find a job in the 1970's, which is why you can find there today our own Fred Wertz, who remains a professor there. Wertz studied at Duquesne under the same professors as Romanyshyn. And Romanyshyn planted himself at University of Dallas, which like Duquesne, is a Catholic University. Duquense University was founded by the Holy Ghost Fathers who, in turn, are linked to a specifically Dutch tradition of phenomenology and social ethics that can be traced back to the same forefathers.

It was through the vehicle of Fr. Adrian Van Kaam in the 1960's that existential phenomenology and humanistic psychology informed by personalist ethics, became the seed that sprouted the now worldly renowned, unparalleled and finally APA accredited program in clinical psychology at Duquesne University. Duquesne remains to this day the premiere locus of the most innovative and influential scholarship in human science psychology. It is no wonder that such a program would jump at the chance to hire a student of Gordon Allport – Rolf von Eckartsberg – to teach at Duquesne; the kinship there is very clear.

So now we are back full circle:

Leibniz begat Kant who begat Stumpf who begat Allport who begat Von Eckartsberg who begat Romanyshyn who begat Sipiora, as well as another of my teachers at Duquesne, Eva Simms, who begat Robbins, McInerney, Olson, and others involved in the field of humanistic psychology today.

The Dignity of the Person

The roots of personalism are closely linked to Immanuel Kant's distinction between dignity and price. To have a price, according to Kant, was to be measured against other values. A box of cereal and a 1998 Mazda MX-6 are objects, and objects have a price – their worth can be estimated in terms of other values, such as their economic worth. However, a being with dignity must be measured according to her intrinsic worth. "In the realm of ends," he writes, "everything has either a *price* or a *dignity*. Something that has a price can be exchanged for something else of *equal value*; whereas that which exceeds all price and therefore admits of no equivalent, has a dignity" (Kant, 1785, cited in Williams, 2005). To say that human beings have dignity is to say that any given person is beyond price, of non-quantifiable value that is non-fungible and therefore of infinite worth. This is why, against utilitarian ethics, we can say that it is impossible to estimate a person's worth over and against the anonymous crowd. Human worth is not summative in the way something with a price has summative value. Therefore a single person – think for example of Rosa Parks – can be seen, ethically, to have as much value as a whole collective of people who stand against her.

Personalism vs Individualism

It is important that we not confuse personalism with individualism. Personalism was inspired by an attempt to dialectically transcend the false dichotomy between individualism and collectivism, especially its political manifestations in the extremes of liberalism and communism, respectively. French personalists such as Emmanuel Mounier (1989) and Jacques Maritain (1973) were especially instrumental in articulating the political middle ground that understood the person to be always already related but never merely superordinate to the State, or collective. The State, rather, was to strive to protect the fundamental dignity of all persons, and therefore no person could or should be used merely as a means to the end of collective desires. This ethical imperative of personalism therefore puts a check on democratic process and provides legal and ethical boundaries that serve to protect basic human rights. However, the individual as a person only fully comes into being through his or her social relations with others. To be a person is always already to be social; it is always already to be in relation to others. To have rights is to say that in our relations with others, others have a duty to preserve our dignity, and vice versa, we have a duty to recognize and protect the dignity of others. To be a person and to fully realize our intrinsic dignity through action, is to rise up to the call to respond to the dignity of the other. In this sense, my dignity is always bound up with the dignity of others.

While at first glance these ideas may seem far afield of the work of psychologist Robert Romanyshyn, they actually have a genuine kinship and a common root. In *Mirror and Metaphor: Images and Stories of Psychological Life*, for example, Romanyshyn emphasizes the way in which psychological life is given indirectly through the world of others and things. The self, therefore, is not a thing but a process, an opening in the fabric of being such that other people and things can appear as a world. And to witness to this world as it appears is to implicitly recognize, by virtue of this appearance of others and things, who I am as I stand in relation to it. To be a person, for Romanyshyn, is always already to be in relation, but a relation that can never be reduced to either side of the equation – that is, neither merely lived body nor world, but the dynamic relation between these. I only discover my "I' through my relations with others and things. To be an "I" is to have one's self given indirectly through the images my participatory imagination brings forth as I engage with things and others in projects that matter to me. In this sense, the human psyche has a metaphorical structure. Just as a metaphor is a kind of understanding that appears between two things ('man is a wolf,' "Mussolini is Hitler's tool' etc), so also, psychological life appears in the mirroring relation of self and others.

Agency and Responsiblity

Romanyshyn's work shares with personalism an emphasis on agency and responsibility. For example, in his standout essay "The Despotic Eye: An Illustration of Metabletic Pheomenology and Its Implications," Romanyshyn (2008) writes:

> If as cultural therapeutics, metabletic phenomenology invites and even forces us to remember that what we experience is also a way of experiencing, if, for example, metabletic phenomenology allows us to remember that the body as an object of technological vision is also a way of envisioning the body, then the consequence which follows is that we as humanity are responsible for what we see and what we say. We are responsible for our visions which become incarnated as the visible cultural world. We are responsible for the ways in which we imagine, dream, envision, and build the world. (pp. 524-525)

In this essay, Romansyshyn performs a cultural therapeutic act by showing the connection between linear perspective vision and a culture heading toward disaster – the atom bomb and ecological catastrophe. Linear perspective as a way of seeing is discovered to be a disincarnated, or disembodied, way of seeing that attempts but ultimately fails to escape the finitude of the flesh and earth. This way of seeing provides a context in which it becomes all to easy to view the earth and the body as resources to be used up and destroyed, as if this did not implicate our very survival. To recognize the danger of this vision, and attempt to change it, is within the capacity of humanity, and not only that, it is an ethical imperative.

Like the personalists held, metabletic phenomenology stresses that the person's nature is intrinsically social. The person never exists in isolation, and moreover, persons find their human perfection only in communion with other persons. Interpersonal relations, consequently, are never superfluous or optional to the person, but are constitutive of his inherent make-up and vocation. This kind of relation is proper only to the person. Personalism has endeavored to highlight this aspect of personhood and bring it to the fore. This insight is central to personalism's reaction against and endeavor to overcome the polarization of individualism on the one hand and collectivism on the other. Personalists consider the human being as a 'being for others.' Relationship is not an optional accessory for the human person, but is essential to her personhood. We are each a being-for-relation.

To be responsible, or to be an agent, therefore, is to carefully attend to how one stands in relation to others and the earth. How we constitute the world through our experience is decisive for how it appears, and how the world appears through our constitution of it, influences how we respond to it and who we become in that response. Thus every perception and every action is, in a real and concrete sense, an ethical stance.

Influence of Paul Ricoeur

The fruitful dialogue between Romanyshyn and personalism should be developed in future scholarship, beyond the sketch I have painted here. One of the most important figures, who promises to bring out the important interrelations between Romanyshyn's metabletic work, hermeneutics, ethics and personalism, is that of Paul Ricoeur. Ricoeur was influenced by the French personalists Gabriel Marcel and Emmanuel Mounier and was a regular contributor to the personalist publications, *Esprit* and *Le Christianisme social* (Williams & Bengtsson, 2009).

Romanshyn (2001) is especially indebted to Ricoeur for his approach to metaphor, which provides the framework for his approach to phenomenology in *Mirror and Metaphor: Images and Stories of Psychological Life*. But Ricoeur shares with Romanshyshyn and the personalists an emphasis on agency, and in particular, in the context of his work, an understanding of agency as a dialectic between facticity and possibility.

Agency for Ricoeur (1966), as for Romanyshyn, is never merely freedom without constraint. Rather, the involuntary and the voluntary stand in a relationship of reciprocity. The significance of needs and habits, for example, only come fully into being through their relationship to the will which they solicit and which, in turn, chooses, moves, and adopts them by consent.

Ricoeur's work also shares the central theme of hermeneutic phenomenology, which is at the heart of Romanyshyn's opus. Within Romanyshyn's work we can see that he adopts at times both the hermeneutics of faith and suspicion which, as identified by Ricoeur (1977), is a hermeneutic approach exemplified by psychoanalysis and depth psychology. The psychodynamic, depth oriented aspect of Romanyshyn's (1989, 2007) work is especially evident in his book *Technology as Symptom and Dream*, which interprets technology as a symptom, and his book, *The Wounded Researcher*, which examines the unconscious, depth oriented nature of scholarship. He also places a heavy emphasis on psychological life as metaphorical and narrative, a theme that also permeates the work of Ricoeur.

Finally, like the personalists, we must not forget that all of these scholarly pursuits have as their telos a social ethics. For Romanyshyn, he asks us to consider how our way of seeing in our technological age may already be setting us up for destruction, and a destruction that we must answer for. And Ricoeur, among other things, examines the conflict between love and justice, which demands a poetic resolution, which he discovers by reading the golden rule dialectically through the love command (see Hall, 2008, for a review of this aspect of Ricoeur's philosophy). That is to say, to "do unto others as one would have done to herself" can only ever be fully understood in relation to the command to "love one's enemy," which sets up a paradox that only poetry can resolve. Romanyshyn (2000) too sees himself as failed poet who uses the poet imagination as a form of transcendence. And this, perhaps beyond all other aspects of his work, gives us hope that even as failed poets, we can strive to speak the paradoxical and impossible truth by which ethics, as first philosophy, paradoxically becomes a possibility.

References

Allport, G.W. (1937). The personalistic psychology of William Stern. *Journal of Personality*, 5(3), 231-246.
DeCarvalho, R.J. (1991). Gordon Allport and humanistic psychology. *Journal of Humanistic*

Psychology, 31(3), 8-13.

Dougherty, J.P. (2003). *Jacques Maritain: An intellectual profile*. Washington, DC: Catholic University of America.

Flader, J. (May 6, 2012). Can atheists go to heaven? *The Catholic Weekly*. Online: http://www.catholicweekly.com/au

Greeley, A.M. (1976). Council or encyclical? *Review of Religious Research, 18*(1), 3-10.

Hall, W.D. (2008). *Paul Ricoeur and the poetic imperative: The creative tension between love and justice*. SUNY Press.

Maritain, J. (1973). *Person and the common good*. University of Notre Dame.

Mounier, E. (1989). *Personalism*. University of Notre Dame Press.

Ricoeur, P. (1966). *Freedom and nature: The voluntary and the involuntary*. Northwestern University Press.

Rogers, C.R. (1979). The foundations of the person-centred approach. *Education, 100*(2), 98-107.

Romanyshyn, R.D. (2000). Psychology is useless; Or, it should be. *Janus Head, 3*(2). http://www.janushead.org/3-2/index.cfm

Romanyshyn, R.D. (2001). *Mirror and metaphor: Images and stories of psychological life*. Trivium Publications.

Romanyshyn, R.D. (2008). The despotic eye: An illustration of metabletic phenomenology and its implications. *Janus Head, 10*(2), 505-527.

Scheler, M. (1973). *Formalism in ethics and non-formal ethics of values: A new attempt toward the foundation of an ethical personalism*. Northwestern University Press.

Stein, E. (1989). *On the problem of empathy* (3rd Ed.). ICS publications.

Von Hildebrand, D. (2009). *The nature of love*. St. Augustine's Press.

Williams, T.D. (2005). *Who is my neighbor? Personalism and the foundations of human rights*. Washington, DC: The Catholic University of America.

Williams, T.D., & Bengtsson, J.O. (2009). Personalism. *Stanford Encyclopedia of Philosophy*. http://plato.stanford.edu/entries/personalism/

Woznicki, A.N. (1980). *A Christian humanism: Karol Wojtyla's existential personalism*. Mariel Publications.

Poetic
Reflections

Gods in the Pus/Pus in the Gods:
The Interaction of Decay and Flourishing

Ronald Schenk

      Psychology is the study of the many ways of the soul and its voices, and phenomenological psychology will always ask, "Who is speaking? With what ear is the hearing occurring?" Alchemy, an ancient field of interwoven theory and practice serving as a counterpoint to Western rationalism, is akin to phenomenology in its representations of the inherent interactive complexity of psychological life. One phenomenon seen in dualistic terms from a rational standpoint is the opposition of flourishing and decay. An alternative perspective seeing the interconnection of the two is presented by alchemy. An alchemical image indicating the interaction of the two psychological conditions sets the tone for the essay. It depicts a reclined figure in demise with an arrow in his heart while a living tree rises up from his genitals.[1]

Biological Decay/Flourishing

      Decay or decomposition is an active process by which organic substances are broken down into simpler forms upon death, giving rise to the science of "taphony" after the Greek word for grave, *taphos*. In humans it occurs in five stages each of which manifests a flourishing of activity within the general process of decay: putrefaction of flesh, bloating with liquids and gases, decay through the feeding of maggots, nurturing of surrounding soil with carbon and nutrients, and increase in natural growth around the existing carcass. Decomposition in human and animal cells also occurs at the site of infection in which a virtual battle takes place ("flourishing" as, etymologically meaning, the "brandishing of weapons") in which immune cells called neutrophils in the blood engulf and destroy foreign bacteria, which in turn release toxins or leukocidins, killing off the neutrophils and forming a viscous pus.[2]

Flourishing/Decay in Physics

---

[1] The films "Taxi Driver" and "Blue Velvet" illustrate this interaction of decay and flourishing literally and symbolically in depicting protagonists in an environment of decay moving psychologically toward the "brandishing" of will and budding of eros.
[2] The word "pus" is related to Lt. *puter* or "rotten," the root of our word "putrid" and further from Sanscrit *puyati,* stink, and the Old English, Gothic *fuls* or "foul."

Focusing further in a micro mode, decay also appears at a subatomic level in conjunction with flourishing in the decomposition of a neutron into a proton. The atom is made up of protons and neutrons in its nucleus and electrons travelling outside of the nucleus. Neutrons are usually bound with protons via nuclear force. When they aren't bound, neutrons are "free" and undergo a form of radioactive decay becoming themselves protons in the following manner: Neutrons consist of elementary particles called "quarks," two designated as "down" and one as "up." In the course of the neutron's travels, the down quark may emit a particle called a W boson, thus the neutron becomes a proton (2 up quarks and one down), while the W boson divides into an electron and an electron antineutrino. At the most subatomic level, flourishing, as a mode of *mulitplicatio*, and decay, a form of *putrefactio* go hand in hand.

How can this interaction be imagined at the most "macro" level of thinking – the nature of the universe itself? It is generally accepted that the universe has been expanding from its inception 10 or 20 thousand million years ago at the time of the "big bang" when it suddenly changed from an infinitely dense, hot mass to a rapidly expanding form. The expansion has been determined by measuring the degree of separation of the galaxies, that is, the degree of decay of the original condition. This idea, in turn, gives rise to the notion that there is a universal tendency toward decay, as reflected in the Second Law of Thermodynamics which states that in any system there is a tendency toward entropy, ie., from order to disorder. The fundamental movement of the universe is then seen as being toward its own death or a flourishing toward decay. Through the most macro mode of thinking, expansion can be seen as inherently interacting with decomposition at the universal level.

Flourishing/ Decay in Myth and Literature

The ancient Egyptians had an underworld god, Ammut, in the form of an amalgam of crocodile, lion and hippopotamus, who sits at the feet of Osiris, Lord of the Underworld, at the time of the soul's judgment. Ammut devours the soul judged unworthy often with slow cruelty reflecting nurturance occurring with disintegration.[3] The Romans placed flowers on corpses, as has been done throughout the ages with graves, signifying a

---

[3] The Egyptians would place a skeleton at the banquet table indicating the presence of decay at the table of plentitude.

flourishing that is active within disintegration. The ancient native Mayans had a god of pus, and legend speaks of Catherine of Sienna, who tended to the ill, as having drunk a cup of pus as a sign of her faith, representing the sustenance (flourishing) she received from tending to infection (decay). The ancient Greek myth of Oedipus and the medieval legend of the Fisher King share a common narrative: the land is in a condition of putrefaction or plague, the answer to a question is needed, and it eventually emerges so that an evolutionary movement may occur.

Dante in his epic poem of visitation to the underworld, *"Inferno,"* descends with his guide, Virgil, through the outer regions of Hell wherein souls must spend eternity actively suffering by means of the very sins they committed in the flowering of their life. The travelers arrive at the realm of incontinent sinners and the circle of the gluttonous imaged in a pit of decomposition - the flourishing of the underworld as a never-ending decay. Here the souls howl like dogs while lying on the putrefying ground as rain beats upon them. Next comes the circle of the wrathful where the water is "the blackest purple," and the souls are "all naked with looks of rage... with head and breast and feet and tearing each other piecemeal with their teeth," (Dante, trans. 1961, pp. 103-105) wrath as a perpetual decomposition of the soul. The two companions then enter Malebolgia— literally, "evil pouches"—the region of willful sinners, souls sunken by their flattery such that they are condemned to languish, covered in mud, in dark waters amidst foul fumes, "plunged in a filth which seemed to have come from human privies" (Dante, trans. 1961, p. 233). In Dante's imagination, the flourishing of Hell reflects the decadent behavior of souls in earthly life.

An atmosphere of moral corruption and infectious rot sensed in the collective is famously expressed in a line fron Shakespeare's "Hamlet": having something to do with "the state of Denmark." The theme of decomposition occurs in tropes throughout the play as an expression of the paradox of the decadence in the false flourishing of life anticipating the decay of literal death. In the beginning of the play Hamlet tells with bitter disgust of his very material being which he desires to disintegrate.

> Oh, that this too too solid flesh would melt,/ Thaw, and resolve itself into a dew!.....How weary, stale, flat, and unprofitable/ Seem to me all the uses of this world!/ Fie on't ah, fie! Tis an unweeded garden/ That grows to seed, things rank and gross in nature/ Possess it merely. (I, ii, 129 – 137)

The final scenes in the graveyard where "Lady Worm" reigns supremely are a climax to a narrative of court and worldly life that is as rotten as the corpses of the dead. In the midst of all the court corruption, the subtle "flourishing" that is occurring is the will and passionate determination of Hamlet to take action (brandish weapons) in revenge.

Organizational Corruption

Hamlet's term "wormwood," a reflection of his sense of the decaying moral foundation of his world, is a metaphor for decadence in collective bodies of every sort from families to corporations to nations.[4] The alchemical *uroboros* indicates the head of the dragon swallowing its own tail, an image of a "body" caving in on itself. Corruption in the corporate, financial, and political worlds of the United States, such as the savings and loan scandal of the '80's, Enron, the Iraq war and the '08 Meltdown are notable for the massive fallout that results from the hubris or bloated condition of directors, managers, and politicians. In these collective instances, as well as at the board and committee levels of organizations, what seems like the "flourishing" of business covers up the deceit and decadence of illegal and inept operations. But within this decay is another kind of production – the growing will of individuals and small groups to oppose the corruption, often with the risk of dire consequences for their station within the collective body.

Images of decay in environments such as city neighborhoods are depicted in images of "urban blight." It is in the very run-down abandoned areas of culture and community that new artistic and urban forms emerge. The flourishing of religious institutions such as the Catholic Church and the veneration of big time sports cover an infestation of power-play through sexual abuse and drug use which nevertheless may generate the active will of victims. Finally, a staple of American story-telling is the underlying narrative of corrosion underneath that cathedral of centrist American values, the nuclear family. Here, the putrefaction of jealousies, envies, and power strivings, as well as physical and sexual abuse and maternal deprivation corrode against the surface polish, until again, the activating energy of personal expression - whether as symptom such as anorexia, delinquency, suicide, alcoholism or domestic violence or as direct individual assertiveness - can find its place.

---

[4] The "rotten state" was literalized in the filthy state of castles and palaces of Europe right up to Versailles prior to the French Revolution where the stench was so bad, Marie Antoinette had to cover her nose. See Mary Hodgson, "Palace Intrigue of a Romantic Variety," *The Wall Street Journal*, 16-17 June, 2012, p. C7.

Individual Psyche

In individual psyches putrefaction is the activation of the emotional inheritance of guilt and shame, the inherent sense of "badness," the bite of judgment which gnaws away within and proliferates. The "decay" and "flourishing" in the individual psyche takes the form of battle, often manifesting physiologically as the immune system and its neutrophils (representations of guilt) versus foreign bacteria or antibodies (representing anger), in bodily areas which carry the stress of vulnerability, especially orifices such as oral and genital, reflecting the head and tail of the mythical, self-consuming, uroboric serpent. Dream images of putrefaction and disintegration include seedy atmospheres, rotting foundations, seeping stench, surroundings of peeling exteriors, and the gradual uncovering of infestation of insects and maggots. The "flourishing" within the decay is the growing energy of assertion that lays claim to ground or space to create and establish a unique frame of mind, a particularity of being, regardless of outside influence.

Worm

In his feigned madness, Hamlet addresses the king in a particularly ruthless wordplay anticipating the king's death, in which he states that Polonius (now dead) is at supper.

> Not where he eats, but where his is eaten. A certain convocation of politic worms are e'en at him. Your worm is your only emperor for diet. We fat all creatures else to fat us, and we fat ourselves for maggots. Your fat king and your lean beggar is but variable service, two dishes, but to one table. That's the end....
> A man may fish with the worm that hath eat of a king, and eat of the fish that hath fed of that worm. (IV, iii, 17 – 31)

Forever and always the lowly worm has been a symbol of the putrefaction of materiality after inevitable death, but also signifying a new potential. Hexagram 18 of the *I Ching* reads, "Work on what has been spoiled," and is accompanied by a container holding breeding worms. Christ is associated with the worm as derived from the messianic Psalm 22 which reads, "But I am a worm as no man, a reproach of men, and despised of the people" (Psalms, 22:6). Alchemy presents an amalgam of Oriental and Judeo Christian wisdom in the saying, "Allow the deposit (in the *vas*) to putrify 40 days (ie., into worm larvae)." In the worm, there is the possibility of redemption. An alchemical image depicts Death blowing a trumpet with a worm emerging.

In the Bible, putrefaction is the work of God through disease - Jeremiah: "He has worn away my flesh and my skin, he hath broken my bones," (Lam. 3: 4); Job: "Vermin cover my flesh, and loathsome scabs; my skin is cracked and oozes pus," (Job 7:5); ...for the sake of redemption – Paul: "It is sown in corruption; it is raised in incorruption" (I Cor. 15: 42). In the gnostic mythic narrative, God appears on earth as the Anthropos, the Son of God, the Original Man who descends into the hyle, the dark matter of earth. God is able to manifest in His earthly form solely as a kind of worm (!!!) which in alchemy finds its container, its own particular "imprisonment," in which it can be crystalized into the larvae of worms and then emerge, changed, as spirit integrated with matter.[5]

In the eye sockets of the skull lie the flowers; in the blossom of the flower sits the skull. In the decay are the gods; in the gods lies decay. The gods work in diseased ways, not for a transcendent, spiritualized redemption, but for change, and it may be a transformation that is not amenable to consciousness. C.G. Jung provides a remarkable quote from the alchemical *Museum Hermeticum,*

> (In the) furnace of the cross…man, like the earthly gold, attains to the true black Raven's Head; that is, he is utterly disfigured and is held in derision by the world, and this not only for forty days and nights or years, but *often for the whole duration of his life* (italics mine); so much so that he experiences more heartache in his life than comfort and joy , and more sadness than pleasure…Through this spiritual death his soul is entirely freed. (1951, pp. 353-354)

An entire human life may be lived as a decaying process unconsciously in

---

5 See C.G. Jung (1951) *Aion: Researches Into the Phenomenology of the Self,* (CW 9ii), Translated by R.F.C. Hull, Princeton, N. J.: Princeton University Press, p. 259. Regarding the core sense of "prison" as a means to redemption, one alchemical prescription is to "Imprison the matter in Hell." In "King Lear," Shakespeare gives Lear his finest moment when he gives up his ill-begotten desire for power and leads his loyal daughter, Cordelia, "Come, let's away to prison/....and we'll wear out packs and sects of great ones" (V, iii, 8-17).

service to the flourishing of something beyond knowing.

What is left is a kind of faith. The interface of decay and flourishing can be seen in the art of waiting as an active passivity and a passive action. In 1923 T.S. Eliot wrote "The Waste Land" which set the stage for the modernist sense of civilization in decay in which he also saw the possibility for a kind of redemption. Twenty years ("largely wasted") later he wrote,

> I said to my soul, be still and wait without hope/ For hope would be hope for the wrong thing; wait without love/ For love would be love of the wrong thing; there is yet faith/ But the faith and the love and the hope are all in the waiting./ Wait without thought for you are not ready for thought:/ So the darkness shall be the light,and the stillness the dancing.......Our only health is the disease. (1971, pp. 126-127)

References

Alighieri, D. (1961). *The divine comedy of Dante Alighieri: Inferno.* (J.D. Sinclair, Trans.). New York: Oxford University Press.

Eliot, T.S. (1971). East Coker. In *The Complete Poems and Plays, 1909-1950.* New York: Harcourt, Brace & World, Inc.

Jung, C.D. (1951). *Aion: Researchers into the phenomenology of the self.* (R.F.C. Hull, Trans.). Princeton, NJ: Princeton University Press.

Inclined toward Ceremony

Joe Coppin

All through his work, and most recently in an article titled, "The Necessity for the Humanities in Psychology: the Psychologist and His/Her Shadow", Robert Romanyshyn (2012) fights for a return of psychology to its deeper context as a study of the lived experience of the psyche, or as he puts it in the title of his first book, *psychological life.* There is a reliable, poetic, and persistent attack on the inclination toward materialism and scientism that characterizes clinical psychology as it is most often understood. Romanyshyn fights for a reconnection to the radically diverse *lifeworld* of the psyche and in order to serve that reconnection we must, he says, return to the Humanities.

In this chapter I wish to begin by wholeheartedly supporting this project. Over and over again, as we review the history of our psychological profession we find it moving away from the messy complexities of the arts, philosophy, myth, religion, poetry and prose--all those necessary venues for deep psychological concern. We have become separated from our nature and it is a wounding separation. So yes, there is an urgent need to reconsider our direction--to reconnect to our complex nature. But here I want to move the argument in a particular direction. In addition to and in support of the humanities, I will make the case that a study of depth psychology must take up the psyche's inclination toward *ceremony* as a means of overcoming the separation and healing the wound.

When we approach the psyche as a poet might, or perhaps as a musician might, there is a natural inclination toward ceremony, toward the sense of needing to move a certain way, to see and to listen with a different quality of attention, to walk or sit with a bit of the dancer in mind.

Ceremony One

By the time he walks into the room some of the audience are milling around wondering what to do, a few are seated chatting, one meets him at the door and says, "ah the maestro appears, fashionably late as usual." He keeps to the rhythm of his entrance but manages a response, "The gift of time, use it well." He moves gracefully to his chair never really breaking stride. Once seated he becomes still, eyes closed, as if lost in thought or is it prayer? After a time he begins to speak and all there listen.

The inclination toward ceremony arises in the fleshy connection between person and world and the paradoxical mix of self and otherness it contains, the very stuff that depth psychologists want to know. Ceremony comes forward as an expression of psychological life and so it is worth noting that, and accepting the invitation to move differently when ceremony is underway.

Let's notice that like the Humanities as a field, ceremony, as a category of experience, has also been put to the sidelines in the context of modern approaches to psychology. It is certainly present in our lives but most often understood in terms of a kind of formality for a specific purpose. Weddings, graduations, inaugurations, and many other ceremonies are carried on but it is the form that shapes meaning and as a culture we tend to forget the transformational value that ceremony carries--and the need for transformation that our inclination toward ceremony implies. Given that we have lost our way around ceremony, that we have allowed it to be confined to form, it is urgent that we remember the ways that it arises quite naturally from the body and in the world. For this purpose there is great value in looking into indigenous situations, by which I mean those situations where people are pervasively involved in a kind of mutual participation with the natural world in which they live--they are a part of it--not separate. But as it turns out this is not an easy move. It will require encountering a sticky bit of unconscious projection that lives in depth psychology and binds us to the very agenda of progress and development that has alienated our field from its ancestral connection to the Humanities. I refer to the significant inclination we see in Jungian psychology, for example, toward a progressive and developmental idea that puts the indigenous situation into a parallel relationship to our unconscious past and warns against it. In his essay, "The Type Problem in Classical and Medieval Thought" Jung says,

> The further we go back into history, the more we see personality disappearing beneath the wrappings of collectivity. And if we go right back to primitive psychology, we find absolutely no trace of the concept of an individual. Instead of individuality we find only collective relationship or what Levy-Bruhl calls *participation mystique*. The collective attitude hinders the recognition and evaluation of a psychology different from the subject's, because the mind that is collectively oriented is quite incapable of thinking and feeling in any other way than by projection. (1971 p. 10)

Levy-Bruhl's term, *participation mystique*, has had an interesting history. Jung, and so many others in anthropology, sociology, philosophy and psychology have used it as a way of drawing a distinct boundary that keeps nonwestern indigenous people relegated to a lower, so called, *primitive* status based on their stronger interest in collectivity over individuality. Often the inclination toward collectivity is characterized as childlike. This hierarchical move has been particularly difficult for Jungians who struggle with concerns about ethnocentrism and unconscious racism. Notable among them is Vine Deloria, a Native American scholar. In his book, *C.G. Jung and the Sioux Traditions*, Deloria helps us sort through the sometimes confusing ways that Jung uses the word, *primitive*, and his frequent reference to participation mystique and the ethnocentric schema of cultural evolution as suggested by Levy-Bruhl. I recommend Deloria's work on this subject as he examines the full spectrum of Jung's attitudes toward the idea of the primitive and the fact that it is given both positive and negative values. In fact Deloria saw what most Jungians see in the way Jung's work inevitably finds itself promoting the values of a return to a more indigenous way of being a person in the world.

> Ultimately Jung realized that civilization, for all its virtues, also came with its curses, and that the remedy at hand was an intimate relationship with the natural world--in other words, living in some measure the psychological life of the "primitive" In that sense, of course, Jung's notion of a healing primitive nature was part of a broader twentieth-century understanding that remains with us today. (2009, pp.62-63)

I have taken this critical turn solely in order to invite our awareness of the paradoxical romantic engagement our psychology has with the primitive, alongside a strong suspicion toward our inclination to remain in vital and primary connection with the unconscious as a source.

We continue to label participation mystique as a mistake made by more primitive people who remain identified with landscape in which they live. But what if participation mystique is another way of understanding many of the finer moves we use as depth psychologists? Moves that help us to enter realms wherein the distinctions between subject and object are marginalized in order to fully appreciate what arises from their conjunction? And what if participation mystique, with its effect of blurring distinctions, is at the heart of effective ceremony?

Anthropologist Colin Turnbull who lived and worked among the BaMbuti Pygmies for many years describes a scene of walking deep into the forest at night, "just at the time that leopards would be prowling about in search of food" (p. 74). The pygmies who were normally quite talkative had grown quiet, but it was not a fearful quiet, rather a serene quiet. He noticed that they were carrying no weapons and seemed almost transformed--almost part of the forest. Later one of them told him. "When we are children of the forest what have we to fear of the forest" (p. 74). A clear example of participation mystique yet something more I think.

It reminds me of my own walking in the forest in a spot where I had seen a mountain lion very early one morning. Then, weeks later, walking in the dark of night, I felt the presence of the lion. I could feel the terror of the what the forest held, but there was also an invitation to enter into a ceremonial relationship with it, to be held myself, to take up the image of Lion and move with it, to move any way that it might move, to become it, or at least to become connected to it through our both being part of the forest. It was a profound transformation and a lesson in how indigenous such psychological moves really are. When I am a child of the forest what do I have to fear of the forest?

It is important to note that Jung, and others of course, are ultimately much more interested in how we engage the unconscious than in judging our participation in it as primitive. Having begun his chapter on childhood education by trumpeting the need for schools to address the child's over identification with the world of the parents, Jung, concludes the chapter by acknowledging the importance of a ritualized connection to the unconscious through dream analysis. He suggests there is a need for re-education of adults who may now be overly imbued with rationality. He tells us that,

> as physicians of the soul we have to turn to the ancient art of dream interpretation. We have to educate adults who are no longer willing, like children, to be guided by authority...we have to teach them to listen to their own natures, so that they can understand from within themselves what is happening. (1954, p. 62)

Certainly and repeatedly depth psychologists work at reclaiming the psychological depth that has been paved over by modern sensibilities. It is not a surprise that we find Jungian oriented eco-psychologists leading the way in this return. Betsy Perluss frames the problem well in her recent article, "Following the Raven: The paradoxical path toward a depth ecopsychology". Here she is working on the problem in the word, "primitive."

> ...to be in a "primitive" state of mind is to be negatively enmeshed with the environment, as opposed to the modern mind-set which is more differentiated from one's surroundings.
>
> But isn't this type of enmeshment with nature what we ecopsychologists are looking to recover.? And don't we want to be so fully engaged with our environment that it actually governs our actions rather that us governing it? And, even more so, isn't our mystical participation with the world exactly that which triggers a sense of the numinous? (2012, p. 4)

Our Western oriented psychology continues to deal with an inherited need to see indigenous modes of consciousness as underdeveloped because they do not necessarily start with the project of ego development. This predisposition alienates us from the rich resources in other approaches, other rituals, and other ceremonies.

The emphasis on consciousness also alienates us from the ways that ceremonies may always be emerging from our deeper nature, arising of their own accord. We may both long for, and be, a ceremony.

Ceremony Two

A very poetic phrase, or perhaps an old story is spoken. All present know it is a repetition, repeated many times over. All present hear it as if for the first time, as if it is new, yet ancient at the same time, and thus a space is opened for timeless meaning.

By ceremony I mean something that we do or *participate* in that transforms time and space and, at least for the moment, removes the separations between person and world so that something necessary can happen.

In her book titled simply, *Ceremony*, Leslie Marmon Silko, a Native American writer who grew up on the Laguna Pueblo in New Mexico tells of the essential and healing force of ceremony, which includes repetition and storytelling in the lives of young men returning from World War II to the reservation. In this story it is clear that the absurd disjunction between *there and then* and *here and now* can only be bridged by the participation in ceremonies and telling of stories which have nearly been forgotten.

I want to bring attention to the small kind of ceremony that comes forth in an instant but in that instant carries a sense of eternal necessity. In Silko's novel, Rocky and Tayo are two half-brothers. Rocky is on his way out of the "backward" indigenous culture of the reservation. Tayo, a "half breed" is struggling to make sense of his heritage and his urge for belonging. The two are standing over a deer they have killed, still warm from living but now becoming food for the people.

> Rocky was honing his knife; he tested the blade on a thread hanging from the sleeve of his jacket. The sun was settling down in the southwest sky above the twin peaks. It would be dark in an hour or so. Rocky rolled the carcass belly up and spread open the hind legs. When Tayo saw he was getting started, he looked at the eyes again; he took off his jacket and covered the deer's head.
>
> "Why did you do that?" asked Rocky, motioning at the jacket with the blade of his knife. Long gray hairs were matted into the blood on the blade. Tayo didn't say anything, because they both knew why. The people said you should do that before you gutted the dear. Out of respect. (Silko, 1977, pp. 50-51)

Silko's writing could make a case for the idea that a truly psychological moment is often more authentically and potently expressed through literature and art than through typical psychological writing. So yes, bring us back to the open and creative landscape of the Humanities where, as Jung would have it, everything belongs, everything can have meaning. And one good way to begin that return will be to remember ceremony, to overcome the fear of falling into a mystical participation with the world we are part of, and hold ourselves open to the ceremonies that unfold in that kind of time and space.

Ceremony Three

The chairs are in circle. It has shifted from lecture to discussion-- time for other voices. The teacher sits slightly inclined, both relaxed and attentive. He leans back and he brings his hands nearly together near his face, each fingertip touching its opposite. Fingers become spires and a dome takes its shape. The effect is to form a kind of container that is both enclosed and quite open. It is calls for, and makes, a space for holding thoughts, ideas, hopes, whatever wants to come in response to what has been thus far. And they come.

References

Deloria, V. (2009). *C.G. Jung and the Sioux traditions.* New Orleans, LA: Spring Journal Books

Jung, C.G. (1971). *Psychological types.* Princeton, NJ: Princeton University Press.

Jung, C.G. (1954). Child development and education, in R.F.C. Hull, Trans., The development of personality (pp. 49-62). N.Y., NY: Bollingen Foundation.

Perluss, B. (2012). Following the raven. *Ecopsychology 4*(3), 1-6.

Romanyshyn, R. (2012). The necessity for the humanities in psychology: The psychologist and his/her Shadow. *The Humanistic Psychologist, 40*(3), 234-245.

Silko, L. M. (1977). *Ceremony.* N.Y., N.Y: Quality Paperback Book Club.

Turnbull, C. (1961). *The forest people.* N.Y., N.Y: Touchstone

Alchemy, The Higgs Boson and Metaphor

Mike Denney

> *When all comes to all, the most precious element of life is wonder.*
> *Even the real scientist works in the sense of wonder. The pity is, when*
> *he comes out of the laboratory he puts aside his wonder along with his*
> *apparatus, and tries to make it perfectly didactic.*
> —D. H. Lawrence (1928)

The roofs of medieval castles were occasionally blasted skyward when volatile mixtures of molten heavy metals, together with chemicals like sulphur, saltpeter, charcoal, and arsenic, violently exploded while being boiled in cauldrons tended by alchemists, who were often in the service of European kings. These royal venture capitalists of their day dreamed of filling their treasuries with precious gold that, according to their mistaken interpretation of the teachings of ancient alchemy, could be manufactured from base metals.

Since ancient times, the art of alchemy was also inappropriately applied to healing practices, the sought after "gold" envisioned as being the *elixir of life*. Heavy metals were mixed into potions to be ingested by human beings in an attempt to cure illness or to promote health and longevity. Again, the results did not always go as planned. It has been reported that, beginning with the Ming Dynasty, a number of Chinese Emperors died as a result of ingesting therapeutic yet lethal doses of mercury and other heavy metals prepared by their alchemists. In the 16th century, when physicians like Paracelsus prescribed alchemical concoctions, it was not unusual for individuals to manifest side effects like skin discoloration, hair loss, memory loss, numbness, paralysis, diarrhea, and vertigo. Continued use of these heavy metals and poisonous chemicals resulted in liver and renal failure, and, ultimately, death from severe bodily wasting. Mozart is said to have died from mercury poisoning as a result of treatment for miliary fever, and Beethoven was bedridden for months before his death as a result, some analysis indicates, of lead elixirs prescribed by his doctor.

On reflection, we may notice that the untoward consequences wrought by each of these two alchemical practices—trying to make gold for wealth and ingesting metals to achieve health and longevity—resulted from a common error: literalizing the metaphor.

The original theory and practice of alchemy was metaphoric. It began in China well before 1,000 BC, then spread to India, the Middle East, and Egypt. The practice was spiritual, represented by the concepts of the Tao, ayurveda, al-kimiya, and the Egyptian god Toth, expressed in the spiritual metaphor "as above, so below." Cooking metals in boiling cauldrons produced multicolored clouds of vapor, swirls of thick liquids, and clumps of new matter, which were viewed as metaphors for the union of matter and spirit.

Medieval texts in this mystery tradition were often written in obscure codes, using Latin terminology both for the phases of changes of metals and for the relationship of humans to the divine—such phases of change as *solutio, coagulatio, sublimatio, putrefactio, and mortificatio.* Most importantly, in the *coniunctio,* the union of opposites, the yearned-for alchemical "gold" was not the literal precious metal, but was a metaphorical symbol for the highest universal truth, the "Philosophers' Stone." Alchemy was, indeed, a sacred task.

One of the early phases of alchemical change was called *massa confusa.* According to the old texts, *massa confusa* occurs in the early phase of change, as metals cook in boiling acids and the rising pungent vapors form a *nigredo* or black cloud above the alchemical vessel. In this "cloud of the unknowing," the alchemist is cast into a state of bewilderment, stripped of intellectual conception, as he awaits the uncertain outcome of this *opus magnus.* In this state of wonderment and awe, the alchemist must hold the tension of opposites, seeking a union, or *coniunctio,* of the heavens with the earth, of matter with spirit.

During the Scientific Revolution, this alchemical path to awareness was thoroughly discredited. In the early 17th century, Rene Descartes was impressed by Francis Bacon's earlier statements, which emphasized that only with an empirical scientific method could human beings "put nature on the rack and torture out her secrets." Descartes told of how he was enamored of oratory and poetry, but that he thought "both were the gifts of the mind, rather than the fruits of study." He took nine years in travel and isolation to meticulously train his mind away from metaphor and the poetic in order to achieve a truly objective frame of mind, a philosophy that knowledge could be gained only through the rational power of human reason.

Ironically, both Bacon and Descartes seemed unaware of their deeper integrations of metaphor and poetics in their own objectivity; Bacon finding meaning by using the metaphors of the "rack" and 'torture," and Descartes referring to "gifts of mind" and "fruits of study."

Isaac Newton, considered by many to be the greatest scientist who ever lived, enjoyed working alone in a private shed experimenting alchemically with gold, lead and mercury. He considered this part of his work to be a "noble" and a "sacred" task, secondary to his pure science.

The dominance of empiricism continued through the 17th and 18th centuries as Boyle, Priestly and Lavoisier gradually conquered the metaphorical connotations of alchemy to beget a science that became modern chemistry, which seemed to rid the mysteries of anything poetic or spiritual.

In 1928, the metaphor of alchemy re-entered modern culture when the empirical analytical psychologist Carl G. Jung received a manuscript, a German translation of an ancient Chinese alchemical treatise entitled *The Secret of the Golden Flower.* Jung's psychology had always included the seemingly innate propensity of human beings to contemplate themselves as a collective in relationship to the divine cosmos. In alchemy, Jung found a new metaphor of the human psyche, stating, "I had very soon seen that analytical psychology coincided in a most curious way with alchemy. The experiences of the alchemists were, in a sense, my experiences, and their world was my world."

Two years after reading *The Secret of the Golden Flower*, Jung began a long journey on a more scientific path toward the union of matter and spirit. In 1930, Jung received in his office at Kusnacht, a new patient named Wolfgang Pauli, a young mathematical genius and quantum physicist who was already a Professor of theoretical physics and destined to be a Nobel Laureate. After Jung meticulously analyzed 400 of Pauli's dreams, the men discussed and corresponded for the next 26 years, letters that are recorded in the book, *Atom and Archetype* (2001). Gradually, the two men came to the conclusion that the human psyche and the material stuff of the universe were one.

Through alchemy, the most ancient of spiritual practices, together with quantum physics, the most advanced and reliable science ever known, Jung and Pauli had found a union of matter and spirit—metaphor and science were in an alchemical and quantum *coniunctio.*

Nowadays, the most profound and existential *massa confusa* of both spirit and science remains: Why is there something rather than nothing?

In his popular science book, *A Universe From Nothing* (2012), theoretical physicist and cosmologist Lawrence M. Krauss, purports to answer that question. After reviewing the history of both our Milky Way galaxy, which contains approximately 100 billion stars, and the nearly 400 billion other galaxies in the known universe, Krauss concludes that it all could only have come into existence from nothing. In the Big Bang, a gigantic explosion some 13.5 billion years ago, there appeared from nothing the subatomic particles called protons, electrons, and neutrons that then formed helium, hydrogen, and lithium, the earliest manifestations of matter. Soon, came the stars, and from their stardust, planets were formed; then the earth gave rise to life forms which, from an anthropocentric point of view, evolved into human beings who are capable of contemplating and manipulating this great universe.

Noting that *nothing* is somehow unstable and can therefore create something, Knauss emphasizes that the metaphor of a creator "God" leads to an *infinite regression* and is therefore unnecessary or at best redundant, calling it, "a rather facile semantic solution to the deep question of creation." Knauss does admit that, "Maybe literally, as well as metaphorically, we are making much ado about nothing." Yet, he fails to mention that the quality of instability is *something* not *nothing*, and thus there remains, still, the mystery surrounding the creation of "nothing." The infinite regression will not go away.

In an earlier book, *The God Particle: If the Universe Is the Answer, What Is the Question?* (1993) by Nobel Prize-winning physicist Leon M. Lederman and science writer Dick Teresi, the historic dream of replacing "god" with science as the path toward answering the existential question of creation is reviewed, from the Greek philosophers Democritis and Heraclitis through the latest in quantum physics. The authors tell the story of British physicist Peter Higgs and other quantum researchers in Belgium and the United States, who in 1964 proposed that the answer to this riddle of creation and existence could theoretically be solved if there existed a special subatomic particle, other than a proton or neutron, that would provide a "symmetry-breaking" effect that would produce "non-zero" matter from empty space (nothing). Thus Higgs and others offered a literal and scientific theory for the union of matter and spirit, the *coniunctio* sought metaphorically by the ancient alchemists.

International teams of scientist set out to discover this subatomic particle. To do so, they built the Large Hadron Collider at CERN

Switzerland, the most powerful particle accelerator ever built, a 17 mile-long tunnel currently operating at only half power, which during every second in time generates more data than exists in all of the world's libraries. These physicists had already decided that, if discovered, the new particle would be named the Higgs Boson, in honor of Peter Higgs.

In the United States, amidst the noise of skyrockets and firecrackers celebrating the 4th of July 2012, the news came from CERN: Physicists had, indeed, discovered the Higgs Boson in their experiments in the Large Hadron Collider. Over the clinking of glasses and celebrations, we were told that this will change our concept of the universe and our place in it. The existential mystery of creation, of the state of being itself, will be solved by the Higgs Boson. Questions about the union of matter and spirit will no longer be necessary.

Still, something nags. What is it that seems to be missing? Has science once again triumphed in our search for meaning, and are we now bereft of metaphor?

The renowned columnist, David Brooks, in the April 11, 2011 edition of the New York Times, published an Op-Ed piece titled *Poetry for Everyday Life*. After reviewing books by linguistic experts, Brooks points out that to adequately express their ideas people use a metaphor every 10 to 25 words. He goes on to say, "Even the hardest of sciences depend on a foundation of metaphors. To be aware of metaphors is to be humbled by the complexity of the world."

Perhaps a more metaphoric look at the Higgs Boson particle is in order. We understand how Higgs became a part of the name of this new subatomic particle, but what about Boson?

Satyendranath Bose is a nearly forgotten hero in this story. He was born in India in 1894, was a child mathematical genius, and in 1924 wrote an important and original paper on quantum statistics, which showed that two protons can be in the same place at the same time. Later, he worked closely in Berlin with Einstein, who immediately recognized that Bose's work was an essential advance toward the development of quantum physics. It is said that Bose deserved a Nobel Prize, though he was never awarded one.

Interestingly, Bose loved poetry, and could recite in Bengali, English, French and Sanskrit. He was a member of the Bengali renaissance, which was presided over by his close friend, the great poet Rabindranath

Tagore, who once wrote a poem praising Bose's strange quantum science. In dialogue with Bose, Tagore found that his poetic expressions of deep and hidden reality were very similar to quantum theory, as they both reveal a universe beyond what appears to be discerned by ordinary logic or science. In their separate works about spirit and matter—Bose in quantum physics and Tagore in poetry—both men were powerfully influenced by the sacred Hindu Sanskrit texts of the Rig Veda creation myths. A few months before his death in 1941, Tagore wrote a poem about creation:

> This gigantic creation
> Is a fireworks display of Suns and stars across the skies
> On a cosmic time scale.
> I too have come from the eternal and the imperceptible
> Like a spark in a tiny remote corner of space and time.
>
> Today as I enter the final act of departure,
> The flame weakens,
> The shadows reveal the illusory character of the play,
> And the costumes of grief and happiness begin to
> slacken.
> I see the colorful costumes left over by hundreds of
> actors and
> Actresses across the ages.
>
> Outside the arena of the theatre
> I look up only to find
> Beyond the backdrop of hundreds of extinguished stars
> Nataraj, silent and lonely.

Nataraj is the name given to the image of the god Shiva dancing on an aureole of flames, with one leg lifted, his four arms outstretched toward the four directions, and balancing over a demon of ignorance. Nataraj is said to perform two dances, the *Tandava*, or violent dance, and the *Lasya*, or gentle dance. The former is the dance of destruction, and the latter the dance of creation.

In this metaphoric frame of reference, we may remember that the Higgs Boson is often referred to as the "God particle," after the title of Lederman and Teresi's 1993 book. But, quantum physicists eschew this characterization, saying that their work has nothing to do with the spiritual, that it offers, instead, a purely objective, scientific, and literal explanation of how something can come from nothing.

And so it is that in our quantum *massa confusa*, we may enter a state of wonderment and awe, as our quantum physicists bring the Large Hadron Collider up to full power, bombarding Higgs Bosons against one another in an attempt to literalize the metaphor, to reduce the God particle to matter. Will they experience untoward reactions, as did those who used alchemy to seek literal gold, health and longevity yet sometimes produced explosions and death?

In our anthropocentric science-fiction story, we might imagine our heroes of literal objective research provoking a new Big Bang, a massive explosion destroying the planet earth yet creating out of nothing still another 400 billion galaxies. In this scenario, our scientific endeavor need not be *either* a dance of destruction *or* a dance of creation. Indeed, we might imagine it to be both—a magnificent *coniunctio*, a metaphorical, spiritual, and alchemical union of opposites.

References

Pauli, W., & Meier, C.A. (2001). *Atom and archetype: The Pauli/Jung letters, 1932-1958*. C.P. Enz, & M. Fierz (Eds.). Princeton: Princeton University Press.

Krauss, L. (2012). *A university from nothing*. New York: Simon & Schuster.

Lawrence, D.H. (1928). *Hymns in a man's life*.

Lederman, L., & Teresi, D. (2006). *The God particle: If the universe is the answer, what is the question?* Boston: Houghton Mifflin Harcourt.

A Letter to Robert Romanyshyn about Orpheus

Thomas Elsner

Dear Robert,

I'm writing this to you in thanks for a wonderful evening last night over drinks, the conversation we had about Orpheus staying uppermost in my mind and heart now the next day. Many thoughts and images have constellated in regard to this myth, a myth so close to you (thoughts that accompany a bit of a hangover from mixing wine and gin!), especially regarding the "backwards glance" in the Orpheus story which, to tell you the truth, has always sort of stood out like a beacon for me as well.

So here's the meaning of it all:

Orpheus is THE artist, poet, musician. He is seeking the soul lost in the underworld. This is like the Persephone myth isn't it? – and Sophia, and innumerable other stories as well, found in alchemy and elsewhere, the soul in fetters or the sleeping beauty, or the white dove hidden in the lead as the alchemists put it. We know that Orpheus was said to have inaugurated all of the ancient mystery traditions – Orphic, Eleusinian – Plato I think, or a neo-platonist, maybe Proclus, traces Plato's philosophy back to these mysteries, which themselves were said to have been founded by Orpheus. Thomas Taylor, the "English Pagan" of the late eighteenth, early nineteenth century who translated the Orphic hymns thought to have been the hymn book for Eleusis, talks about this in his writings.

So, in the Orpheus myth THE artist is in love and has lost his soul. It is as if art is trying to bring up the lost soul through the power, dynamism and sheer longing that is constellated through romantic love and a type of artistic creativity that is centered on romantic love. But romantic love is a "sickness unto death." It leads to death, to the death of the beloved. Romantic love has one focus and one focus only -- the image of the beloved. Hence the turning around; Orpheus cannot help but turn around to see Eurydice– for she is his most important, his ONLY value. And that is meant to tell us that this kind of romantic love alone, and the artist alone, or one could say, the aesthetic consciousness alone, even in its sublime perfection, cannot bring up that lost Sophia, the soul lost in Hades. Almost, but not quite. Orpheus, as an artist, does everything right, unimaginably right, and despite all of his capacity to create beauty, despite all his musical spells, he still loses his soul. I think this is meant to tell us something about the idealization of art, and/or the idealization of the woman as muse. Jung in his own descent to the underworld, described in *The Red Book*, wrote, "First came the image of a crater, and I had the feeling that I was in the land of the dead. The atmosphere was that of another world." He encountered a lost feminine soul in that underworld of his psyche, but resisted her insistence that he was an artist.

For me now the Orpheus myth shows that there must be something else, some other value in love besides the romantic longing for the beloved – Romeo and Juliet, Tristan and Isolde etc. – and some other way of bringing back the lost soul than art. All of the romantic love myths, and this is true for Romanticism in general also, end in death, in a kind of death longing, or a sense that the lovers can only be together in death. Psychologically this implies that in Romantic love the whole problem of the soul remains unconscious. Coleridge, thinking of himself as a poet, recognized that he had a tendency to become addicted to delusion.

If we compare the Orpheus/Eurydice myth with the myth say of Persephone, what is the difference? In the Demeter/Persephone myth it is the power of maternal Eros, not romantic Eros, that at first attempts to bring the lost feminine soul up from the land of the dead. Even that insanely powerful mother love – Demeter for her daughter – one of the fiercest of all our instinctual drives as human animals, is unable to bring her back. Persephone DOES come back, part time as we know, but she does come back, because it is the "will and divine counsel of Zeus" and Hermes, that messenger between the worlds, is the one who can bring her back up. He is not in love with Persephone, neither as a romantic lover nor as a mother, but is acting according to the will of God. Perhaps this distinction between Hermes and Orpheus/Demeter is important. The Eleusinian mysteries were an *imitatio Demeter*; both the men and women who took part in these mysteries would ritually imitate the Mother grieving and searching for her lost daughter. The alchemists also searched for the "white dove hidden in the lead" or the feminine spirit lost in the darkness of matter and the unconscious psyche but it was always only *deo concedente* that the opus might succeed.

It seems that if the Kore comes back up into the upper world again, it is not through either the most powerful and purest form of romantic love alone, or the most powerful and purest form of mother love alone, or the most powerful and purest form of art alone, but also something else is needed in the myths – the will, or the "divine counsel" of God.

Psychologically we think here of the idea of the religious function in the psyche which seeks to act in accordance with the will of the self or the totality and center of the psyche. Interestingly I realize now that this is perhaps what marks one of the differences in the Jungian lineage between Marie-Louise von Franz and James Hillman, where the emphasis is placed – on the artistic function/aesthetic function, or the religious function. That is only my speculation based on their readings and not knowing either of them personally.

What the Orpheus myth means for me at the moment is that to make the anima conscious as a psychological function of relationship to the unconscious, to "bring her up out of the darkness", it seems as if something more than the aesthetic attitude towards the psyche may be necessary, and also that something more than the projections constellated in romantic love might be necessary. Romantic love is a possession really; Orpheus is anima possessed. He cannot choose, he must look backwards, and by this backwards glance he loses his soul. Perhaps that is the spell that he is under, the spell of romantic love, and perhaps that is the spell that must be somehow broken if the anima is to become conscious as an actual reality. Orpheus symbolizes anima possession; the only thing he cares about, his entire world, the motivation for everything, is Eurydice AND THAT IS WHY HE LOSES HER. The anima possession is also pointed at in the myth by the way in which Orpheus dies; he is torn to pieces by maenads. "The unconscious anima is a creature without relationships, an autoerotic being whose one aim is to take total possession of the individual", Jung wrote. Is Eurydice the unconscious anima as Jung understood her? For the anima to become conscious, then, might mean that instead of being a possession she becomes a psychological function, a bridge to the Self, something like a man who goes out into the forest to talk with the spirits. Perhaps the bridge between the upper and lower worlds in these type of myths is symbolized by Hermes who, acting in accordance with the will of Zeus, is an image of the religious function of the psyche that can free the lost soul. Neither Orpheus (romantic love) nor Demeter (maternal love) can do this.

For me it seems inescapable that the Orpheus myth is telling us: "romantic love and art alone cannot save the soul" – ALMOST though! Perhaps one could also say that Orpheus is an image of how life IS, or must always be. But that seems a bit fatalistic to me, and also there are other myths, not only the Persephone myth but images in Gnosticism and alchemy, in which the Sophia, the Feminine spirit lost in the darkness, IS gathered up again. Orpheus is obviously one of those incredibly deep symbols that OF COURSE cannot really ever be explained, but these are the thoughts bouncing around in me at the moment after our wonderful conversation.

Best and THANK YOU for that amazing evening at your home. I had the best time.

Tom

Soul Brother in and out of Academia

David Rosen

    Robert is a mensch who values feelings, especially joy and sorrow. He is a person of the heart (intuition) and head (scholar). He is a wounded healer and researcher. Robert realizes that we all fall apart and reconstitute (death and rebirth). He has respect for the ancestors and the afterlife. He knows about darkness and the light within it. He is receptive, honest, and integrity-full. These are the essential elements of the human connection.

    Initially I got to know Robert through his writings and *The Soul in Grief: Love, Death and Transformation* was (and is) my favorite. Next I am fond of *The Wounded Researcher : Research with Soul in Mind*. Then I met Robert and Veronica at the Second International Academic Conference of Analytical Psychology & Jungian Studies held at Texas A&M University July 7-10, 2005. They were dressed in white like Mark Twain and his lady. Robert attended a haiku workshop that I gave, which is indicative of his openness. Shortly after that Conference I left for New Zealand on Sabbatical at the University of Canterbury in Christchurch. I lived in Governors Bay where I met Lanara (my soulmate) on a bench, after offering her half an apple. It turned out that we had both read *The Soul in Grief* and lots of other Jungian books.

    Then Robert contacted me about his pending Sabbatical in New Zealand. I arranged for him to stay in a friend and colleague's home, which was also in Governors Bay. We stayed in contact and in the fall Quarter (2007) Robert arranged for me to be a visiting scholar & lecturer at Pacifica Graduate Institute. Each time I went to Pacifica I stayed with Robert and Veronica. We laughed so much we cried. It felt so natural that we have been friends and soul brothers ever since. In 2008 we presented a panel on "Honoring the Wounded Researcher" at the Third International Jungian Academic Conference held at the ETH (Federal Institute of Technology) in Zurich, Switzerland. I have fond memories of our work together and sitting out in the garden behind the hotel one evening with my students and Jungian colleagues drinking whisky and having a deep and humorous discussion.

    In 2009 I married Lanara and we bought a house in Eugene, Oregon. Robert and Veronica have visited us several times and we always have beautiful and heartfelt conversations. After another Sabbatical at the

University of Oregon in 2011, I retired from Texas A&M. Since I do not have an older brother, I now view Robert as that plus a dear friend. And a good friend is a second self.

Full moon--

owl on branch

waiting to leave academia

The New Rime of the not so Ancient Mariner: a Dialogue with Robert Romanyshyn on Orpheus, Eurydice and Metaphor

Susan Rowland

> It is an ancient Mariner,
> And he stoppeth one of three.
> `By thy long grey beard and glittering eye,
> Now wherefore stopp'st thou me?...
>
> ---
>
> And through the drifts the snowy clifts
> Did send a dismal sheen:
> Nor shapes of men nor beasts we ken -
> The ice was all between.
>
> S.T. Coleridge, "The Rime of the Ancient Mariner"

Robert Romanyshyn went to Antarctica and came back with a story in images. Today we are the "one of three" that "stoppeth" before his presentation of "Antarctica: Inner Journeys in the Outer World" (DVD with music and commentary, 2010). In this paper I want to offer another context to the Antarctica images in relation to Romanyshyn's work on alchemical metaphor and the Orpheus myth of research described in his powerful book, *The Wounded Researcher* (2007). In effect I want to explore the relevance of metonym as well as metaphor for the "Inner Journeys" DVD. I then suggest that the perspective of metonym may point to other aspects of the myths of research.

Robert Romanyshyn's Wounded Researcher as Orpheus

> In this book I am adopting an imaginal view of the research process and I am suggesting that the myth of Orpheus and Eurydice is the archetypal background for how research becomes psychological. The myth of Orpheus and Eurydice is about this process of losing and finding, about this work of transformation in which the other

> becomes a psychological reality, a matter of soul. The work one is called to do is an *other*, and in the process of being claimed by it, of falling in love with it, we learn – by losing it, by letting go of it – to love it for what it is in itself, in its own virginity. (Romanyshyn, 2007 p. 59)

Romanyshyn's *The Wounded Researcher* is a groundbreaking book that returns a wholeness of psyche to scholarly research. His imaginal envisioning of research following the Orphic path of love, loss, descent and losing again is a way of restoring the embodied psyche to the pursuit of knowledge.

Not all valuable knowing is the walled within the domain of the ego or its modern form as intellect or reason. One way of understanding how narrow are modern academic prejudices about knowledge, is, as *The Wounded Researcher* demonstrates mythically. Elsewhere I have explored the mythic context of research in terms of the gendered creation myths of consciousness best offered in *The Myth of the Goddess* (1991, Rowland, 2012). Authors Baring and Cashford argued that human consciousness is formed through founding mythical structures, encountered in Western culture historically through ancient animistic Earth based religions, supplanted by "sky father" monotheisms. These two types of myth can be characterized as myths of separation from the other, *and* myths of consciousness based upon embodiment and connection. Western modernity suffers because of its long suppression of the latter variety of consciousness, which is identified as feminine and "nature" through a dualism erected by privileging the sky father. 'He" creates matter and earth as "other" to "his" transcendence, so becoming as a consequence, feminine and inferior.

Such endemic psychic structuring pervades the kinds of research and knowledge privileged in the Western academy. The polarized mode of sky father knowledge is based upon separation from the other, just as the sky father created nature as separate from himself as disembodied mind. Putting aside the fantasy of a researcher as mind wholly transcendent of bodily matter, we know that even research for disembodied reason requires the body and the passions to feed the energy of this product of 'pure' mind. Through the story of Orpheus and his descent to the underworld, Romanyshyn returns us to a wholeness of psychic endeavor in the making of knowledge.

The Wounded Researcher shows that research can be based upon *connection* to the whole embodied psyche and its powers of imagination.

This, I believe is what Romanyshyn is getting at when he discusses the research process as imaginal and requiring a myth to *figure* it out, to be a figure for *us* to follow into the dangerous underworld of psyche. In fact, the crucial dynamics of the Orpheus marriage are an opportunity for sky father and earth mother to find a new rapprochement. Orpheus loses Eurydice to death. She disappears into Hades and finally his laments are so heart-rending that he is permitted to follow. He can take her back into life only if he walks out of Hades never turning back. He turns back and she is gone forever.

Romanyshyn characterizes this loss superbly as averting the danger of smothering the other in research. If we have a truly ethical, loving, psychically healthy relation to the other as our research; that which we are *called* to do, then we have to learn to let it go, *to let it be in its own place.* Another way of looking at the necessity to both nurture and let go is that we have to learn to embrace *both* sky father separation and earth mother connection to the research. We are therefore called upon to create as both sky father and earth mother, as making something separate from ourselves *and* with an organic, erotic connection to our body and soul.

So the researcher as Orpheus finds Eurydice in that which he is called to love, nurture, unite with, feel the loss of, quest into Hades for, and lose again. In this Orpheus lives the fate of Romanyshyn's related work on metaphor. He undergoes and alchemy of body and soul.

Alchemical Metaphors

The Wounded Researcher restores the place of the underworld to the making of knowledge and meaning. The underworld demands to be included because it is the "other," the unconscious part of the psyche. It is dark, shadowed and feminine to a culture dominated by sky father structures distorted into patriarchy. Of course the underworld of dreams, nature as other, death, the embodied unconscious is always feminine as in the Earth Mother, yet "she" is not feminine to the exclusion of the masculine for she is prior to the division into genders. She is anima in *animated matter* and depth psychology knows that she matters.

At one level, as I have argued before, Earth Mother's psychic potential is expressed as animism and returns to us in the body of literature (Rowland, 2012). Art imbued with the *whole* psyche offers *animated* reading and writing. Whereas our culture privileges the writer as an 'author' as *authority* over the meaning of a text, reading for the whole psyche liberates many voices. A writer can be a jealous sky father trying to maintain his monotheistic grasp upon the (otherwise) dead matter of words. Or, a writer can embrace some potentials of the Earth Mother and see the multiplicity inherent in words as the essential *animation* that bodies language by embodying it in us.

Romanyshyn in his earlier wonderful book, *Mirror and Metaphor: Images and Stories of Psychological Life* (1982), expresses this animistic liberation as metaphor.

> A metaphor, we might say, is an explicit psychological act, while psychological experience is a living metaphor…. [M]etaphor and psychological life do share the same function. (Romanyshyn, p. 199)

Metaphor liberates meaning from a fantasy of literalism into the plurality of imagination. It animates texts into animism. Metaphor, as Romanyshyn shows, is the psyche truly alive.

Here also metaphor is the psyche in alchemical mode for it can be understood as textually enacting alchemical processes of *solve et coagula*. Traditional alchemy described repeated operations of making liquid solutions to merge substances, followed by distilling them into a solid powder or identity again. "Solve et coagula" signifies "dissolve" (solve) and harden into shape (coagula). These fundamental chemical processes can be equated to the way a metaphor works mentally to dissolve or undo the identity of a thing by perceiving it in terms of an-other.

Metaphor dissolves, yet also "coagulates" because it does not destroy the original entity. Rather in a metaphor like "the moon sailed the sky," moon is momentarily dissolved into a ship yet is restored *differently*. The *solve et coagula* of metaphor leaves a psychic trace on our understanding of this moon in this sky. Here is a powerfully potent example of alchemical hermeneutics in which the alchemy of metaphor unites symbol to psyche by means of poetic processes.

The Ancient Mariner as "a" Personal Myth and Metonym

Here I want to associate Romanyshyn's potent work on the Orpheus myth of research and alchemical metaphor with Jung's key term in *Memories, Dreams, Reflections* that of "personal myth" (Jung, 1963, p. 17). For personal myth comes to stand, metaphorically, for Jung building his whole psychology out of a "solve et coagula" immersion and separation from his own embodied experience including a descent to the underworld.

Jung develops this metaphor as psychology and psychology as metaphor in composing his "personal myth." Jung brings back this metaphoric gift from his underworld as if it was the pomegranate seeds he ate there, so changing his life forever. For him, the metaphoric mode is narrative, and hence the "myth" in "personal myth." His use of words like "shadow" and "anima" are metaphoric and psychological in Romanyshyn's sense when framed in the perspective of Jung's personal myth, the life story *experienced, embodied, lived, suffered, celebrated.*

Here I want to link up Romanyshyn's alchemical metaphor to a related notion around the figure of metonym. So "personal myth" is *personal* because it is a lived bodily narrative. Yet Jung also uses the term to denote the stem, perhaps the unseen core, of his psychology as a system of thought offered to the world. Jung openly avows what is often alleged about one person generating a theory; that Jung's psychology as a system is based upon Jung's psychology as a man. Where an accusation of personal material might be used as a criticism, Jung regards it as a strength. For not only is psychology an exploration of the interior and one's own inner world is the only one immediately available, but Jung shows in *Memories, Dreams, Reflections* how integral contact with the underworld is to his theory.

In these senses, Jung's psychology is an alchemical metaphor of his descent *and* a metonym because it is also and embodied *continuity* between his underworld experience and his future work. Metonym is where the part stands for a greater whole. Metaphor ends by separation so emphasizes sky father consciousness; metonym instates and preserves *connection* with the other so belongs to earth mother. Put another way, Jung's descent has a metonymic figure in an-other myth. Wrenched into hell, Jung becomes Persephone; one who has no choice about entering the underworld and only returns by accepting a permanent connection to it.

Abducted by Hades, Persephone is so mourned by her goddess mother, Demeter that the gods permit her return. And yet this particular descending researcher has ingested some of the dark. An alternative to the final parting of Orpheus and Eurydice is Persephone's *repeated descent* for some months of every year because she has eaten some of the food of the underworld. Yet her sojourn is not without significance for when with Hades she is his Queen. As a power with the dark, Persephone aids Eurydice when appealed to when she wishes to return with Orpheus.

Jung brings back his alchemical metaphoric gift of his psychology from his underworld; it becomes the singing of Orpheus heard throughout the world. Yet *Memories, Dreams, Reflections* shows how it also contains the pomegranate seeds he ate there, changing his life forever. Here he is also the Persephone and metonymically embodied within his research.

One might be tempted to argue that the tragic story of Orpheus and Eurydice provides a masculine sky father myth of research and Persephone a feminine, and earth mother version. However such a dichotomy is potentially misleading because here neither "masculine" nor "feminine" are essentialist descriptions of gender. Nor do they exclude each other. Both women and men can research as Orpheus and as Persephone.

As stated earlier, the brilliance of *The Wounded Researcher* is its expansion of research to the *whole* psyche including an embodied connection to the other, Eurydice. Rather these two myths of research together with their two figures of metaphor and metonym are gendered in the sense that sky father and earth mother are archetypal ways of being that haunt the Western mind. While Orpheus's underworld adventure ends on a sky father trope, Eurydice's collaboration with Persephone re-minds us of the unknowable energies of the unconscious psyche. Demeter is evidently a goddess devoted to her role as *mother*, yet Persephone's metonymic fate releases the feminine from too much literalism in embodying earth mother consciousness.

Persephone finds a way of privileging earth mother metonymic connectivity without literally giving birth. One could call this a metaphor! Romanyshyn shows the metaphoric sensibility as the true psychology; Jung calls it "personal myth." I want to add the possibility that we can *also*, as well as read our-selves *metonymically* as expressing an ecological vision of humans *within* nature. For on the one hand in metaphor, we need to see ourselves as separated from the underworld in order to allow "the work" its freedom from our ego concerns. On the other hand, metonymically, we also feel underworld nature *within us* as those pomegranate seeds.

Turning to the images of "Antarctica: Inner Journeys in the Outer World" we see those seeds begin to sprout. Here this (not so ancient) mariner can share his images that are both alchemically coagulated from (metaphor) and metonymically embodied in that inner journey into the outer lands of ice and snow. This "rime" we need, now.

I am honored to have this chance of engaging with the ground *breaking* and ground *fertilizing* work of Robert Romanyshyn.

References

Baring, A. and J. Cashford. (1991). *The myth of the goddess: evolution of an image.* New York and London: Vintage.

Coleridge, S. T. (2007) "The rime of the ancient mariner" in S.T. Coleridge and William Wordsworth. *Lyrical ballads.* New York: Penguin Classics. (Original work published 1798)

Jung, C. G. (1963/1983). *Memories, dreams, reflections,* Recorded and Edited by Aniela Jaffe, London: Fontana.

Romanyshyn, R. (1982). *Mirror and metaphor: images and stories of psychological life.* London and New York: Routledge.

Romanyshyn, R. (2007). *The wounded researcher: research with soul in mind.* New Orleans: Spring Journal and Books.

Rowland, S. (2012). *The ecocritical psyche: literature, complexity evolution and Jung.* New York and London: Routledge.

Runaway Train

Glen Slater

> *"You do what you have to do, and I'll do what I have to do. Whatever happens, happens."* Oscar "Manny" Manheim

The phenomenologist and depth psychologist Robert Romanyshyn has declared the 1985 thriller *Runaway Train* his favorite film. Given his roaming interest in the arts, expertise on imagination, and not infrequent imbibing of two or three films at a stretch, this perplexing choice cries out for understanding. And this collection of essays in his honor presents the perfect opportunity to risk a ride on his cinematic train of thought.

At first glance this story of a hardened criminal's escape from an Alaskan maximum-security prison appears no more than a well-realized tale of pursued liberty and recovered dignity, wrapped up in an admittedly arresting human duel with the icy elements. The film may well have planted a seed for Romanyshyn's recent jaunt to Antarctica. But one might be forgiven for wondering whether his inner Ebert stands on frozen tundra or skates on thin ice. Yet, as it turns out, we don't need to go too far beneath the surface of the phenomenologist's choice flick to find hidden value. Oscar "Manny" Manheim's (Jon Voight's) quest for freedom aboard a quaternity of unleashed locomotives contains an existential subtext that reverberates right along with the thunder of the diesel engines. The film happens to have some heft. As we might actually expect from a script penned originally by Akira Kurosawa and brought to the screen under the direction of Andrei Konchalovsky, it's psychologically nuanced and aesthetically biting. Indeed, *Runaway Train* belongs to a cinematic rare species: the meaningful action film. Yet, understanding where my colleague's ideas and eccentricities track with this work still presents an intriguing challenge.

Let's step back and pan around. Romanyshyn's love of film certainly dovetails with his psychological and phenomenological perspective. Cinema at its best conveys precisely what his work seeks to describe—the "imaginal world . . . the invisible that subtends the visible world" (2002, p.xx). Depth psychology, especially that of Jung, attends to unconscious dynamics and archetypal configurations; phenomenology locates depth and essence in appearance. In combination these fields allow us to appreciate the way psyche is revealed through what appears on screen. In seeing a film "we enter a realm closer to the dream than to waking life, a place where the raw, subversive, and sublime can come to light." (Slater, 2005, p.2).

Cinema, by nature of the medium, is forced to display and embody thought and emotion. This process converts objective things into the kind of presences Romanyshyn has called the "subtle bodies of the imaginal realm, which are between mind and matter" (2002, p. 90). Specifically, cinematic vision is formed through a rendering of *visual metaphor*, whereby a setting, situation or gesture simultaneously carries the literal narrative and conveys a deeper soul story. A sense of metaphor draws out the poetic composition taking place in the entire filmmaking process, wherein setting, camera angles, lighting, gestures and dialogue work together to lift a veil on the character of Being. It's this layering of elements that captivates us, drawing us into multiple levels of meaning and significance. At the same time, in a finely wrought cinematic moment, the lines between the unique and universal, profane and sacred break down. And when this metaphorical quality is most potently present, it is, as Romanyshyn has stated in broader context, "a small miracle, a momentary tear in the fabric of the quotidian round, a moment when a vision which erupts between us is neither a psychological experience nor a material event." The outcome is an "empathic attunement to the world." (2002, p.103).

Film, literally projected, conveys a world in which a psychology of projection gives way to a world of enchantment—a state of animation in which we "watch the forms of transcendence fly up like sparks from a fire" (Merleau-Ponty, 1962, p. xv). The medium allows us to overcome the tendency to divide inner and outer, recover a sense of the 'sympathy of all things,' and perceive the dream body even in gritty, worldly dramas. A strong cinematic vision provides a haven from the modern technological habit of transforming "the self into a spectator, the world into a spectacle, and the body into a specimen." (Romanyshyn, 1989, p. 33). A gifted actor, for example, divulges the overlap of body and soul, reminding us of being "bodily creatures with a carnal knowledge of the world" (p. 38). Further, by following a protagonist through trials and tribulations, we come to see outer events and persons as manifestations of interior dynamics, especially in the arising of shadow, fate, and calling. By obliterating the line between character and embodied circumstance, film prompts us to imagine life as a mythic drama, in which we must endeavor to play the role given to us with as much heart as possible.

Runaway Train conveys these cinematic qualities by turning an autonomous machine monster into an unstoppable vehicle for movement in the main character's psyche. The train begins as a means of outer escape but turns into that which drives his emerging quest for inner freedom. The landscape through which it careens becomes indistinguishable from the iced-over antagonism of the world he must confront, within and without, in which his challenge is to kindle a small flicker of humanity.

The film begins with the protagonist winning a civil rights case and a reprieve from three years of solitary confinement in "the hole," a cell that had been welded shut after two previous escape attempts. In the eyes of his fellow prisoners, Manny's defiant survival and resilience to the system makes him *the man,* and the film proceeds to reinforce the feeling he carries a part of them all, as well as the essential human struggle to preserve spirit and self-respect. The prisoner's struggle comes into focus through his confrontation with Warden Ranken, who refers to Manny as "an animal" and to the rest of the prisoners as "mostly animals" or "pieces of human waste." Ranken, having failed to break Manny in the hole and thereby crush the will of his fellow inmates, becomes hell-bent in his quest to destroy the man. After he orchestrates a stabbing attempt that leaves a Christ-like wound through Manny's hand, the warden only galvanizes the convict's defiance of tyranny.

In fitting irony, the man regarded as human waste makes his escape first at the bottom of a cart of dirty laundry and then out through a sewer. Finding freedom through full immersion in underworld bile becomes a key motif in the film. Buck (Eric Roberts), a boxer who's all bravado and no backbone, aids the breakout. When Manny reluctantly allows Buck to follow him he gains a sidekick and foil to his character. After stripping down to apply a layer of grease and cling wrap, Manny takes off like there's no tomorrow, down the pipe, into the river and out into the snow-covered plain; Buck settles into his pattern of looking for a way around every necessary hurdle. Buck's big and strong but isn't tough or smart. Manny's the man with a damaged eye and scars to the face; Buck's the pretty boy, in spite of his boxing exploits. Manny knows how to wade through the sewer of life; Buck's just beginning.

After a quick defrosting and change of clothes in the empty locker room of a rail yard, the pair climb aboard the ambling group of locomotives at the same moment the sole engineer has a heart attack and tumbles out of the front cab. Buck asks, "Why that one?" Manny replies, "'Cause I want it." Now they're left to their devices and begin a battle of wits, figuring out how to get off an accelerating behemoth and on with their lives. With the brakes burnt out and the seemingly unreachable lead engine running the show, they're on the move and facing their options.

In what is arguably the pivotal scene of the film, Buck starts to fantasize about another cash-grabbing, quick fix while Manny sees straight through him and offers a devastating pushback.

BUCK

You know, I spend almost every night of my life dreamin' about this kind of shit.

MANNY

Dreamin'? (Spits). Dreamin'. That's bullshit. I'll tell you what you gonna do. You gonna get a job. That's what you gonna do. You're gonna get a little job. Some job a convict can get, like scraping off trays in a cafeteria. Or cleaning out toilets. And you're gonna hold onto that job like gold. Because it is gold. Let me tell you, Jack, that is gold. You listenin' to me? And when that man walks in at the end of the day. And he comes to see how you done, you ain't gonna look in his eyes. You gonna look at the floor. Because you don't want to see that fear in his eyes when you jump up & grab his face, and slam him to the floor, and make him scream & cry for his life. So you look right at the floor, Jack. Pay attention to what I'm sayin', motherfucker! And then he's gonna look around the room - see how you done. And he's gonna say "Oh, you missed a little spot over there. Jeez, you didn't get this one here. What about this little bitty spot?" And you're gonna suck all that pain inside you, and you're gonna clean that spot. And you're gonna clean that spot. Until you get that shiny clean. And on Friday, you pick up your paycheck. And if you could do that, if you could do that, you could be president of Chase Manhattan... corporations! If you could do that . . .

BUCK

Not me Manny. I wouldn't do that kind of shit. I'd rather be in fuckin' jail.

MANNY
(Wistfully)
More's the pity, youngster . . . more's the pity.

BUCK
Could you do that kind of shit?

MANNY
I wish I could . . . I wish I could . . .

Manny's had time to figure out redemption will be found in that place where the shadow is eaten, the place where passions and reactivity are metabolized and turned into resilience and resolve. He's come to see "the gold," not as an outer material quest, but as the outcome of a process that begins by transforming primary urges. And as we come to see, this recognition portends the outcome of the film.

Events take a turn when they look out of their cab and see a figure making its way toward them, perilously negotiating the iced-over gangways and couplings. After jumping the interloper, they find themselves in the presence of a young woman, Sara (Rebecca DeMornay), a rail yard hostler who had fallen asleep in a recessed compartment. She brings with her both knowledge of the train and a mirror for the men's confrontation with their own integrity. Sara's an uncorrupted, fresh-faced reminder of the life beyond egoic self-concern. As an unwitting muse, her mere presence will provide both men a way out.

After several rounds of conflict, the three become one, bonded by circumstance. Manny knows what must be done. He makes a final leap onto the lead locomotive and loses half his fingers in the process. Meanwhile, Warden Ranken cannot suppress his need to destroy Manny and all he represents. He drops from a helicopter onto the train, which has now been rerouted towards a dead-end. But Manny overpowers Ranken and handcuffs the warden in the cab of the lead locomotive, effectively reversing their roles and revealing their respective states of being. When Ranken insists they're running out of time, Manny muses, likely recalling his three years welded shut in solitary confinement, "We've got all the time in the world."

The smashed cab of the lead engine now becomes a crucible where the warring splits between human and inhuman, altruism and self-preservation, liberty and constraint are melted down. Ranken, failing in his plea to be unshackled, begins his verbal assault: "You're scum." Manny replies, "We're *both* scum, *brother*." Immediately the train ploughs through two grated barriers; the prison bars, long left behind in actuality, are now psychologically dashed as well. When Ranken pushes on, challenging Manny's ability to find freedom or win the circumstance, Manny drives home his new state of mind: "I *am* free, Ranken, I *am* free." He then releases this Zen-like observation: "Win, lose, what's the difference?" The quest for external liberation has given way to inner release. He's now driving the train.

Ranken lives in a divided world in which the "animals" must be caged and the "humans" must control them. But in this splitting he becomes the very thing he despises. He can only imagine the situation in the most literal terms, seeing neither his own imprisonment nor the redemptive possibilities in those he has locked up. He doesn't know the difference between personal freedom and physical liberty. But the moment Manny points to his head and announces, "It's all up here," the convict transcends his literal circumstance and enters a realm of existential choice.

From this emancipated position, to Vivaldi's Gloria in D, Manny makes his way to the back of the lead engine and decouples the remaining, powerless locomotives, which begin to slow to a halt. Buck and Sara, now saved, implore him to stop the entire train, which is within his power. Instead, Manny climbs to the top of the still charging locomotive and leans directly into the wind, snow, and ice. He's become one with the circumstance and with his own nature, and the whiteness that would take his life now seems to purify his soul. The film flashes on the faces of his fellow prisoners, looking out beyond the bars of their cells. With Ranken still chained below, the pair disappear into the mist.

In *Runaway Train* the world *worlds* and the soul ensouls. Romanyshyn, savvy to the way technology, earth, destiny and ethics crisscross our being, knows exactly where this train heads and why it can't be stopped. Indeed, his writings and teaching are a testament to the soul's trials and triumphs and the thin line between them. He savors this film for its revelation of the way imaginal realities carry the psyche-world relationship. His affinity for frozen landscapes no doubt adds to the mix, as does the distant echo of his oft-repeated desire to exchange professorship for bus driving. We should watch out! Moreover, one cannot help but notice, there's more than a passing physical resemblance between Robert Romanyshyn and Oscar Manny Manheim—sans the scars and bad teeth. Add in the Brooklyn accent they share in common and I think we've discerned just how this film transports my friend to some of his favorite places.

References

Konchalovsky, A (Director), & Globus, Y. (Producer). (1985). *Runaway train*. [Film].
    (MGM Home Entertainment)
Merleau-Ponty, M. (1962). *The phenomenology of perception* (C. Smith, Trans.). New York:
Routledge.
Romanyshyn, R. (1989). *Technology as symptom and dream*. New York: Routledge.
Romanyshyn, R. (2002). *Ways of the heart: Essays towards an imaginal psychology.* Pittsburgh:
    Trivium Publications.
Slater, G. (2005). Archetypal perspective and American film. *Spring*. Vol. 73.

Poiesis of Soul: *Revisioning Psychology* As Mythical Method

Dennis Patrick Slattery

> Every text reveals the weaver's predilections (Preface, *Revisionng Psychology ix)*.

The beauty and complexity of James Hillman's *Revisioning Psychology* (1975) rests substantially in how it creates a new metal from an amalgam of poetics, mythos and archetypal psychology; its consequence is iconoclastic, insightful and innovative for anyone interested in the cross currents of poetry and psyche. Where the two converge to converse is one landscape where myths have their genesis.

I can remember so many evenings in the early years of the Dallas Institute of Humanities and Culture when James stood at the podium and dazzled us with his reading of a fairytale or reworked a passage by Jung or entered into a reverie on some cultural phenomenon, like the importance of culture for the health of the city that he wanted us to see with new eyes. Only the literary critics and theorist, Louise Cowan, to my mind, carried the same intense cache of dazzle at that same podium; both were in some sense mirrors of one another as innovators of vision and as instigators of a deepening imagination, which is where their individual works united most forcefully and most fruitfully, for me. I don't think I am alone on this point.

Revisioning Psychology carries the same innovative and epic heft as Herman Melville's *Moby-Dick (*1851/1977*)*, with all the complexity, episodic turns of plot, meditations on the soul of matter and the mothering of soul that the earlier American writer, steeped in the same waters of archetypes in his whaling voyage, invited on board the Pequod. The white whale, for James, is the psyche itself—seductive, slippery, sagacious, serious, serene, twisted like the crooked lower jaw of the elusive whale, fierce in its seduction, oblique and occupying all latitudes at once. Moreover, like the white whale, soul itself in James' lexicon is the *anima mundi*, the world soul, which only the deepest philosophic and poetic meditations are capable of grasping.

We each comprise qualities of the figures of Ahab in his quest to disarm what cannot be affected, really; Ishmael in moments of quiet reflection when something subterranean reveals itself in a breach of imagining; a bit of Stubb who wants to seize the whale as a commodity and pin it to the main mast of nature or cut a slice and have it served raw on a dinner plate; and even a seasoning of young Pip, who, upon jumping from the whale boats not once but twice and is thereby abandoned to the sea's immensity. Alone amidst the vastness, Pip, "carried down alive to wondrous depths, where strange shapes of the unwarped primal world glided to and fro before his passive eyes; and the miser-merman, Wisdom, revealed his hoarded heaps; and among the joyous, heartless, ever-juvenile eternities, Pip saw the multitudinous, God-omnipresent..." (1851/1977, p.443). Pip's watery epiphany reveals to him the largeness of the soul in the waters of the mind and matter and speaks from that day forward a foreign language comprehensible only to divinities that stir in the deep.

Sometimes I think that James is most like Pip. It is as if he jumped from the boat chasing whales and entered the immemorial immensity of the ocean to imagine with new eyes the mythic creatures swarming there, where, as he writes, "The being of a thing is revealed in the display of its *Bild* (image)" (1981, p. 29). However, unlike Pip and more akin to Ishmael, James survived the vision to give us the story of that deep diving in *Revisioning Psychology*, his legacy and, as history is certain to affirm, his most original sea voyage and from which all other soul explorations emanate.

Its waters are vast and deep, its themes enormous and universal. Ishmael observes at one point in the voyage: "To produce a mighty book you must choose a mighty theme. No great and enduring volume can ever be written on the flea, though many there be that have tried it" (1851/1977, p. 487). Choosing mosquitoes or flies will not carry the load. *Revisioning Psychology* shows clearly in its wake the leviathanic theme of the soul itself—not only the individual soul we are personally guided by, but the *anima mundi* herself. His vision, moreover, is that large, that epic, and so has the capacity to engage one of the grand cargoes of this inclusive genre: re-founding old verities into a new order of understanding. Only a few souls will and have been called to exact the courage to explore such a region that stretches both horizontally across the landscape of history and downward mythically to the depths of pathology, affliction and woundedness itself.

Lyn Cowan, a Jungian analyst and no lightweight in her own books on the soul, related to me in an email not long ago, that it was she who, working closely with James in Zurich in the 1970s, typed the manuscript of *Revisioning* and created the index from the galleys. One evening over dinner, after the manuscript had been shipped out to Harper's Publishing in New York, she told James: "You know, it's your masterwork. You'll never write anything that reaches this level again." He looked startled and then reflective and said: "Yes....you're probably right" (email: 11/14/2011, 9:03 A.M.). Privileged to be so close to every word of the work as she typed them, I imagine her musing on what was unfolding before her with each click of the keys and then as she constructed the index for it, another form, perhaps, of the "Extracts" of *Moby-Dick* and the *prima materia* of the entire opus. Getting to know Lyn recently, and agreeing with her assessment of James' opus, I realize what can and does happen to readers of a writer's work: they can in moments of clarity, see as readers more deeply into it than can the work's creator and thus have the advantage of fathoming depths of the work of which the writer is unaware. Such is the power of *Revisioning's* mythic enormity.

Revisioning is a work that taught me it must be read slowly and meditatively, a few pages each morning. In the fall of 2010 when I entered ¾ time employment at Pacifica Graduate Institute and so would not be flying out for two week stretches between August and January, I was drawn, after 30 years had passed, to re-read and take slow notes in my own hand, not computer-generated, of so many passages that had puzzled me when I was a graduate student at the University of Dallas when James taught there. I recall at that time how little money my wife Sandy and I had. I could not afford to buy the book, so I checked out a copy from the library and took it to my night job as a Pinkerton Security guard at Delta Steel in Dallas.

There, after much sleuthing at 1 or 2 in the morning, I succeeded in locating the key to the Xerox machine, a fairly new invention at the time in the mid-70s. Under cover of guarding the offices and rolls of sheet metal pressed for buildings to be constructed across the United States, one night I copied, accompanied by great glee and a little fear, the entire book, a Xerox I still possess as a memento of those leaner but nonetheless abundant years of study. I can still recall the strongly-worded memo of outrage that went out to all employees from the company's president, demanding to know who it was that made so many copies on the machine, an expense he could do without and perhaps the employee to boot. I kept my head down, beyond suspicion; what in heaven's name would a security guard be doing making copies of something at night? I hid neatly under the stereotype, safe behind my shiny Pinkerton badge. That is how I procured my first copy of *Revisioning:* by theft. I never told James that story; now I wish I had. I think he would have been delighted to learn that Hermes was alive and active, as James himself carried that Hermes energy through every page of *Revisioning*. Stealing *Revisioning* was as deliciously psychological a move as reading it.

Recovering the Soul

James' work, you may remember, is divided into four sections: 1. Personifying or Imagining Things; 2. Pathologizing or Falling Apart; 3. Psychologizing or Seeing Through; 4. Dehumanizing or Soul-Making. The structure is his own genre wheel of the soul and perhaps they could with beneficial effect be seen as analogies of the four genres—lyric, tragic, comic and epic—(1984/1992/2003) worked out so elegantly in Louise Cowan's genre wheel. Something of these respective quaternities, as C.G.Jung noticed repeatedly, offer images of wholeness and completeness.

In each of these sections he wrestles with, so to realign the work of psychology—the logos of the soul—with the imagination, something lost, he affirms, with the development of psychology along the sluices of fantasies, burdened as they are with naturalism and scientism. A too literal reliance on one's history flattens the power of the imaginal life into insignificance. Moving between a phenomenology that returns us to the lived experience of an event and an imaginal mythology that seeks primarily through afflictions the movement of the soul to a fuller awareness of itself, *Revisioning* recalibrates the nature and purpose of psychologizing as a form of mythologizing. Its overarching aim regarding psychology James is very clear about when he affirms in a Preface to the 1992 edition: "to revert its vision to poetic principles and polymorphic Gods... of ensouling the nonhuman" (1992, p.ix). Each section of his quaternal structure can stand alone, but each also assumes a deeper richness when placed in relation to the others.

My interest warms up considerably over the last part of section Two: Pathologizing or Falling Apart. It is most interesting right now for a couple of reasons: 1. It most intensely expresses some of the major terms for one to discover through uncovering layers of one's personal myth; 2. It rests heavily on the seminal movement of *reversion* essential to archetypal psychology's mythical method, namely, a return to the origins, through memory, of one's life story. It also *clarifies* further the nature of fantasy not as make-believe but as the presence of analogy, metaphor and what Jung earlier called the "als ob" or "as-if" nature of our psychological turn (1970, par.315). It further highlights the central act of pathologizing, what James calls an "iconoclasm; as such it becomes a primary way of soul-making. Its method is to break the soul free from its identification with egocentric seeing through the upperworld heroes of light and high Gods who provide the ego with its models...and have cast our consciousness in a one-sided, suppressive narrowness regarding life, health and nature" (1975, p.89). Finally for my purposes, it asserts as well what James calls the "polytheistic perspective," which David Miller was to successfully amplify later in his book, *The New Polytheism* (1974).

Revisioning Psychology's Mythical Method

Almost ten years after the publication of *Revisioning Psychology,* James was to return to mythos and plot in one of his most popular books, *Healing Fiction,* my second favorite of all of his works, after *Revisioning.* There, early on, he proposes a startlingly new way for us to understand the plot of a story when he outlines Freud's seminal contribution to psychology, both positive and negative. Freud's theory of the Oedipus story became the foundation for his theory of human development or its absence, in the form of libido. James observes: His [Freud's] double style of writing required that what was plot and myth on one level was theory and science on another" (1983, p. 11). James' quarrel with Freud's theory is not that it fails as an empirical hypothesis of human nature, but that it fails poetically; it is in essence neither deep nor embracing enough nor an "aesthetic enough plot for providing dynamic coherence and meaning to the dispersed narratives of our lives" (p. 11). In the last qualifier, note in passing the polytheistic method appearing in the phrase, "dispersed narratives."

The four modes of consciousness that comprise the large sweep of James' mytho-poetic method mentioned earlier might be taken up individually in a series of lecture-discussions and meditated on slowly so to see the whole through each of these rich and episodic parts.

Pathology offers pathways to the soul's deepest nature and temper. Recognizing our own form of pathologizing is an essential dimension of gaining a fuller self-consciousness, for "pathologizing is itself a way of seeing; the eye of the complex gives the peculiar twist called 'psychological insight'" (1975, p.107). Eyeing pathos is another vision of gazing at the soul through the analogy of affliction. I want to suggest that in our afflictions prowl the deepest plots of our unfolding fiction. The archetypal dominants of these fictions are the stories embodied in myths. *Revisioning Psychology* involves rereading mythic stories as analogies of the soul in its suffering. Remembering the mythic plots is an imaginal and archetypal method of recollecting ourselves: "we could look at the high-flying young champions—Bellerophon falling from his white winged horse, Icarus plunging into the sea, Phaethon hurtling in flames, unable to manage his father's chariot of the sun—to understand the self-destructive behavior of the spirit... (p. 103). Herein the mimetic marriage between mythopoiesis and soul-making is made present; both share a love for the imagination's power to make present what would perhaps lie under the floorboards of consciousness, lessening our ability to live more fully, more poetically, which is to say, more psychologically.

References

Cowan, L. (1984). Introduction: The comic terrain. Louise Cowan (ed.) *The terrain of comedy*. Dallas: The Dallas Institute of Humanities and Culture.

Cowan, L. (1992). Introduction: The epic as cosmopoesis. *The epic cosmos*. In J. Larry Allums (Ed.), *The epic cosmos*. Dallas: The Dallas Institute Publications.

Cowan, L. (2003). Introduction: The tragic abyss. *The tragic abyss*. In Glenn Arbery (Ed.), Dallas: The Dallas Institute Publications.

Hillman, J. (1975). *Revisioning psychology*. New York: Harper Perennial.

Hillman, J. (1981). *Thought of the heart*. Eranos Lectures 2. Dallas: Spring Publications.

Hillman, J. (1983). *Healing fiction*. Woodstock, Connecticut: Spring Publications.

Jung, C.G. (1970). *Aion: Researches into the phenomenology of the self*. Vol. 9, 2 of *The collected works of C. G. Jung*. Trans. R.F.C Hull, 2nd ed. Princeton: Princeton University Press.

Melville, H. (1851/1977). *Moby-Dick, or the whale*. Introduction by Clifton Fadiman. Illustrations by Boardman Robnison. Collector's Edition. Norwalk, Connecticut: The Easton Press.

Miller, D. (1974). *The new polytheism*. New York: Harper and Row.

Presences are more than Cognitions: Pathways through Phenomenology to Poetry[1]

Les Todres and Kathleen Galvin

> When we speak are we speaking up for the things of the world, giving voice to their desires, breathing with them in a con-spiracy of dreams? Is this our vocation, which we have lost, and for which we silently grieve as do the things of the world?
>
> —Robert Romanyshyn (2002, p. 65).

Introduction

We are particularly interested in how poetry and phenomenology can come together to increase understanding of human phenomena. And further, we are interested in how these more aesthetic possibilities of understanding can occur within a community context: the possibility of a form of scholarly hospitality in which understanding is shared through an ongoing process of embodied and communicative participation. In this way, phenomenologically- oriented understandings may meaningfully speak of what is common between us as well as what may be uniquely lived for each of us in terms of its individual context and nuance. We thus ask: Could one direction for phenomenology be a project that leans towards the *awakening of presences in shared communities of understanding*? We thus offer a meditation on the nature of understanding in embodied, shared and participatory contexts by drawing on a philosophical foundation that includes Gadamer, Gendlin, Levinas and Shotter. Building on these foundations, we reflect on the challenge of 'awakening presences' as an aesthetically-oriented community challenge.

Philosophical Foundation

> Presence: an intangible spirit or mysterious influence felt to be present. (Websters Dictionary, 2008)

Philosophically we have drawn on Gadamer (1975/1996), Gendlin (1992) and Levinas (1961/1969) to characterize three very important dimensions of embodied relational understanding.

---

[1] This chapter is a shortened and revised version of a journal article which originally appeared as Galvin, K., & Todres, L. (2012). Phenomenology as embodied knowing and sharing: Kindling audience participation. *Indo-Pacific Journal of Phenomenology*, 12 (Special Edition, July), 9 pp. doi: 10.2989/ IPJP.2012.12.1.9.1122

From Gendlin we have drawn on the importance of one's embodied self that gives a meaningful reference to "owning" understanding, so that the understanding becomes full of personal, historical, and tactile references. In line with this emphasis, it is only the "epistemic body" that is adequate for gathering together the whole sense of something in a felt way. This "whole sense of something" is never a "frozen" or finished whole, but is open: an alive presence which is always on the way.

From Levinas, we have taken the importance of being open to the other, and all the meanings there – what it takes to be deeply informed by "the that" of the others alterity or difference that is always more than we can know, thus stretching us to horizons beyond ourselves.

And Gadamer helps us to see what understanding is: a play between embodied self and other. In such a play or open dialogue there is a care for the presencing of the phenomenon, such as "the loss", "the comfort", the "shimmer" that will always be more than just you and me – it is always *that*. "That" is always more specific and more complex than any generalisation.

Gendlin, Levinas and Gadamer together have challenged us to engage in the kinds of understandings and communications that can respect the full spectrum of self, other and world without fully reducing one to the other.

Therefore in "embodied relational understanding" (Todres, 2008) we find a tension between our shared vulnerable heritage (our embodiment) (Galvin & Todres, 2009), the infinity of otherness (alterity) and the alive more of the phenomenon that wants to announce itself.

This challenges us with the question of what kinds of discourse are adequate in keeping this alive tension that is contained in embodied relational understanding. Here, we see poetry and poetic discourse as a medium that can swim in this space between sharedness, otherness and the quality of "just this thing" (the loss, the comfort, the shimmer).

In the context of seeking the spirit of the participative creative process we also wish to consider the task of what Gendlin (2004) has called "Carrying Forward", in his "philosophy of implicit entry".

Within this perspective, 'carrying forward' is a crucial part of what happens qualitatively in the space where shared meaning is transmitted and evolves between us. This communicative space is more than just me and you in an embodied way, but also includes where we are culturally, historically and beyond this, from domains of possible meanings and horizons that transcend all the patterns we have made of them.

In relation to our concern to kindle aesthetically-oriented, embodied relational understanding, we wish to offer a particular type of carrying forward: a carrying forward of embodied meanings in a way that can "move" or "touch" another, and from there, be offered again to "touch" another and so it goes. In this way of carrying forward one is not simply duplicating the meanings that are transmitted to us. Rather we are participating in meaning making – receiving something "old", but also bringing something "new". So, in this "carrying forward" we wish to care for the other and what he or she is telling us about "that". But we are also, as participants, taking part in how these meanings relate to us personally and how they carry a certain aliveness "of that" as they move into the future.

This aliveness of the phenomenon, "the that", is alive in the sense that it guides the embodied interaction, and the whole process has qualities similar to what Gadamer called "a conversation". Wallulis, a scholar of Gadamer, has written about the notion of a "language community" and how meaningful conversations are "grabbed" by the matter at hand, in a community context, far beyond the individual partners construction of it:

> This event of conversation is not led by any of the partners but rather by the subject matter (*sache*) of the conversation that "seizes" the conversation partners into the process of coming to an understanding. (Wallulis, 1997, p. 274)

Thus in the process of carrying forward, phenomena or "that", have the characteristics of a kind of presence that is alive, and it is this presence that also changes in some way as we embody it both personally and as a community.

A further implication of this kind of carrying forward is that it is never a linear or abstract process because it is grounded in the rich multiple textures of the embodied world. And it is these rich multiple textures that are far more alive than any thought that represents them. So:

> …there is, for Gendlin a "carrying forward" of the body that has been "dogmatically hidden" by conceptual thought (Wallulis, 1997, p.275).

This presence, although carried by words is always more than the words. In any alive language "*the more*" stays alive as a reference for it and continues to act as a source of further words between us. In this respect Gendlin highlights the crucial role that the body plays in nourishing the kind of language that is 'up to the task' and 'alive enough' for embodied relational understanding. He says of carrying forward: "it is not only the *words* but also *what we want to say* to carry *the situation* forward,… in a *bodily sensed way*" (Gendlin, 1992, pp. 102-103).

In this process there is a creative tension between self, other and the alive phenomenon. The tension means that no words can ever be the final words, but words can open a space and move us toward a new understanding Therefore we engage in this tension in a bodily felt way; we are carrying forward by engaging in the tension between what is shared and what is other. As such, the essence of language is not in its summative power, but is in its opening power, and our participative quest is to use language that is able to move within this "open". Foti (1997) indicates how, for Gendlin, language is always tactile and full of sedimented meaning:

> Gendlin points out that *every* use of a word has, in fact, a certain metaphoric force because, whenever a word is brought to speak, its sedimentated meaning and connotation intercross with the speakers' sense of the context or situation. (p. 310)

Within such a tactile sense of bringing something to words one may notice that this sense is *more than* any particular phrases or words that one uses about it, and that the tactile sense is a living thing (presence or phenomenon) that feeds and sustains the meanings. We see poetry as one potential way that such presencing can be awakened and sustained, and Renga (an interactive form of poetry writing), offers a way to engage audience participation. In concrete terms this kind of carrying forward then requires a play between an attentiveness to the phenomenon there, given by the other and the community of others, and our own sense of being touched bodily, and further, making something of the presences that have been gifted us. It is with these understandings that we have become interested in Renga as one possible participative process that could address the following practical question: How can we kindle embodied and linguistic participation in a way that holds sharedness, otherness and "the that", and does so in a way that can move within the 'open'?.

A Participative Poetry Writing Process: Kindling Audience Participation

We have been intrigued by the Japanese form of Renga as one possible cultural process that can facilitate the awakening and sharing of presences,. Renga is a Japanese form of shared poetry that generated the later form of Haiku (Reichhold, 2008). At a symposium in Canada, Kate engaged the audience in a process of writing Renga. The audience comprised qualitative researchers from the discipline of education and literary poets.). We refer readers to a longer paper (Galvin & Todres, 2012) for a description of what happened, and a reflection on the benefits and challenges of this way of engaging in the awakening and sharing of presences. At the end of the process, there was an acknowledgement of the power of the experience for its palpability: how the presence of the phenomenon was bigger than any words could say; how the meanings were not as much in the words but in the palpable presence of something' almost in the room.'

The "That'" That Moves

A paper by Shotter (2003) entitled "Real Presences: Meaning as living movement in a participatory world" has inspired us to think even further about the ontological depth of 'sharing'. Shotter speaks of the emergence of "dynamically unfolding structures of activity that we all participate in 'shaping', but to which we all must also be responsive in giving shape to our own actions"(p. 435). In his articulation of the nature of "real presences" as an alternative to "mental representations", Shotter indicated to us how what is shared in sharing meanings, is potentially much more palpable and complex than an interpersonal process in which one person conveys meaning to another. There is a third thing, and in a sense it has its own body. And more than this, it has "life" in that it moves and changes beyond the participants. Its reality is neither dependent on construction by the actors present, nor is it completely independent of the actors present. "That" and we, move together, interdependently. For Shotter, real presences are "incarnate in the folding activity in which we ourselves are participants" (p. 461).

At the same time these real presences "can, like another person issuing instructions and commands, exert a communicative influence on us and thus (at least partially) structure our actions" (p. 462).

We would like to say that our process of kindling audience participation through Renga is one way in which meanings as moving presences ('the that' that moves) can potentially inform the possibility of shared and palpable embodied relational understanding.

Conclusion

Phenomenology, in its quest to access lived meanings in a meaningful way may benefit from more consideration of how presences become more alive as we attend to them, not only with linguistic hospitality, but with bodily hospitality as well. We thus argue that the central spirit of phenomenology is to proceed on the basis of an epistemology where understanding is never cognitively alone, but always intertwined with its senses, moods, qualities and multiple intersubjective and cultural contexts that are given to consciousness in the ways they are holistically presented. So, being present in this phenomenological way is never only "cognitive presence" or "aesthetic presence" or "emotional presence". We derive these specialised presences rather than originally live there. This means that the awakening and sharing of presences is much more than the exchange of information or cognitions, and such an acknowledgement within scholarly discourse begins to restore the poetic truths about how we dwell within the intimacies of this vast mysterious world that we claim to know, package and use.

References

Foti V.M., (1997) Alterity and the dynamics of metaphor In D.M. Levin (Ed.) *Language beyond postmodernism: Saying and thinking in Gendlin's philosophy*. Evanston, Illinois, North Western Press.pp.305-320.

Gadamer, H-G., (1975/1996). *Truth and method*. London: Sheed and Ward. (Second Revised Edition, Originally published in German in 1965.)

Galvin KT & Todres, L (2009) Embodying nursing openheartedness: an existential pespective. *Journal of Holistic Nursing* 27 (2), 141- 149.

Galvin, KT & Todres, L (2012). Phenomenology as embodied knowing and sharing: Kindling audience participation. *Indo-Pacific Journal of Phenomenology. 12 (Special Edition, July: Evidence Based Pedagogy)*. 9 pp. doi: 10.2989/IPJP.2012.12.1.9.1122

Gendlin, E.T., (1992) Thinking beyond patterns: Body, language and situations. In B. de Ouden & M. Moen, (Eds.), *The presence of feeling and thought*. New York: Peter Lang

Gendlin, E.T., (2004) The new phenomenology of carrying forward. *Continental Philosophy*

Review. 37 (1), 127-151.

Levinas, E. (1961/1969). *Totality and infinity* (Trans. A Lingis). Pittsburgh, PA: Duquesne University Press.

Reichhold, J., (Ed.) (2008). *Basho: The complete haiku.* Kodansha Europe.

Romanyshyn, R (2002). *Ways of the heart: Essays toward and imaginal psychology.* Pittsburgh, PA: Trivium Publications.

Shotter, J. (2003). Real presences: Meaning as living movement in a participatory world'. *Theory and Psychology* 2003, 13, 4 435: 468

Todres, L.(2008) Being with that: The relevance of embodied understanding for practice. *Qualitative Health Research, 18* (11) 1566- 1573.

Wallulis , J. (1997) Carrying forward: Gadamer and Gendlin on history, language and the body. In: D.M. Levin (Ed.), *Language beyond postmodernism: Saying and thinking in Gendlin's philosophy.* Evanston, Illinois,North Western Press).

Websters Third New International Dictionary (2008) Merriam Webster, U.S.

Contributors

Stephen Aizenstat, Ph.D., is the Chancellor and Founding President of Pacifica Graduate Institute. He has explored the power of dreams through depth psychology and his own research for more than 35 years. His Dream Tending methodologies extend traditional dream work to the vision of an animated world where the living images in dream are experienced as embodied and originating in the psyche of Nature as well as that of persons. His work opens creativity and the generative process. Dr. Aizenstat's book, *Dream Tending*, describes multiple new applications of dreamwork in relation to health and healing, nightmares, the World's Dream, relationships, and the creative process. His other recent publications include: *Imagination & Medicine: The Future of Healing in an Age of Neuroscience* (co-editor with Robert Bosnak); "Dream Tending and Tending the World," in *Ecotherapy: Healing with Nature in Mind*; "Soul-Centered Education: An Interview with Stephen Aizenstat" (with Nancy Treadway Galindo) in *Reimagining Education; Essays on Reviving the Soul of Learning; The Soul Does Not Specialize: Revaluing the Humanities and the Polyvalent Imagination*, with Dennis Patrick Slattery and Jennifer Leigh Selig: "Depth Entrepreneurship: Creating an Organization out of Dream Space", in *The Transforming Leader: New Approaches to Leadership for the Twenty-First Century; and "Fragility of the World's Dream"*, in *Eranos Yearbook 2009-2010-2011 Love on a Fragile Thread*. For more information, visit www.dreamtending.com.

Roger Brooke, Ph.D., ABPP, is Professor of Psychology at Duquesne University, where is also Director of the Military Psychological Services. He is an Affiliate Member of the Inter-Regional Society of Jungian Analysts, and is a Board Certified clinical psychologist. From 1994-2007 he was Director of Clinical Training at DU. His formative professional years were in South Africa in the 1980s, where he was on faculty at Rhodes University, Grahamstown. He is author of *Jung and phenomenology* (Routledge 1991/ Trivium 2010) and contributing editor of *Pathways into the Jungian world* (Routledge 1999). Since childhood he has visited the African bush as often as possible. Home page: rogerbrookephd.com.

Scott D. Churchill earned his doctorate at Duquesne and is Professor and Graduate Program Director for the Psychology Department at the

University of Dallas, where he was hired by Robert Romanyshyn three decades ago. Professionally focused on the understanding of various forms of expression in humans, apes, and the arts, he is well published in the area of phenomenological and hermeneutic methodologies, and has taught a wide variety of courses ranging from primatology and projective techniques to cinema studies and Daseinsanalysis. In addition to developing the notion of "second person perspectivity" in relation to qualitative research, ethology, and health care, Professor Churchill has been a local co-ordinator for Jane Goodall's *Roots & Shoots* and a film and performing arts critic in Dallas since the mid-1980s.

A Fellow of the American Psychological Association, Churchill currently serves on its Council of Representatives and is a Liaison to the APA's Science Directorate and Editor-in-Chief of The Humanistic Psychologist. He is a Founding Member of the new Section for Qualitative Inquiry in the APA's Division of Measurement Statistics, and Assessment as well as a Past President of the Society for Humanistic Psychology and former Secretary-Treasurer for the Society for Theoretical and Philosophical Psychology. He has served as a Visiting Professor at Duquesne, Saybrook, Pacifica, Macquarie (in Sydney), Johannes Guttenberg University (Mainz), the University of Konstanz, the University of Bari, and has recently given a series of master classes at Molde University College (Norway), Aarhus University and Aalborg University (Denmark).

Joe Coppin is a depth psychologist and psychotherapist as well as a teacher and writer. He is the co-author of *The Art of Inquiry: A Depth Psychological Perspective* and he has been on the faculty at Pacifica Graduate Institute since 1996. In the ensuing years he has taught many courses in clinical psychology, archetypal psychology, and research, both in the US and abroad. He has authored new curricula for depth psychology and was the founding chair of graduate degree programs in Depth Psychotherapy and in Depth Psychology with Emphasis in Somatic Studies. He credits his times studying, and exchanging ideas, with Robert Romanyshyn for much of the inspiration and direction that informs his approach to teaching, and to psychological life in general. In fact, the article he has contributed to this volume derives first from his appreciation for the ceremony that comes forth when a very good teacher engages the practices of thinking, teaching, and writing from a place of deep love for the ideas and respect for the people who work them.

Mike Denney, M.D., PhD. graduated from medical school at the University of Michigan in 1959. After nearly a lifetime of practicing, teaching, and writing as a trauma surgeon, Mike went back to school at Pacifica Graduate Institute, and earned a PhD degree in depth psychology. His books are *Second Opinion; Tending Body and Soul*; and his memoir, *Nobody's Boy*. He has also published extensively in scientific journals and popular magazines. Mike is adjunct faculty at the California Institute of Integral Studies and at Pacifica Graduate Institute. He writes and teaches about his passion for the union of science and spirituality in the healing arts.

Thomas Elsner, J.D., M.A., Jungian analyst, is a core faculty member at Pacifica Graduate Institute. He has a private practice in Santa Barbara, California. A former attorney, Thomas trained at the Jung-Von Franz Center for Depth Psychology in Zurich. A member of the C. G. Jung Study Center of Southern California, his areas of special interest include alchemy and the depth psychology of folklore and literature.

Kathleen Galvin is Professor of Nursing Practice in the Faculty of Health and Social Care, University of Hull, United Kingdom. While practicing as a nurse she undertook a PhD study concerning the evaluation of nurse-led practice using conventional research methods. This drew her towards qualitative research and reminded her about her formative literary–rich education in Ireland and what had been lost in her specialized nurse education: a more 'nourished' scholarship that incorporates the literary traditions, story, poetry and reflections on experiential meaning. Observations in clinical practice at that time sensitized her to the reductionist nature of practice in contrast to the depth and detail of what people go through in suffering and in illness. She came to realize that knowing what to do in practice as a nurse didn't always come directly from a technical perspective; rather it came from somewhere deeper and she became fascinated with what this 'deeper' could mean. This led to conversations with colleagues about existential issues and phenomenology and to the work of the human science community

Veronica Goodchild, PhD, is Senior Core Faculty at Pacifica Graduate Institute where she has been teaching since 1999. Educated at London University in her native England, and Columbia University in NYC,

Veronica has practiced as a Jungian-oriented psychotherapist for over 30 years. She is the author of two books: *Eros and Chaos: The Sacred Mysteries and Dark Shadows of Love* (Nicolas-Hays, Inc., 2001, 2008), and the newly published *Songlines of the Soul: Pathways to a New Vision for a New Century* (Nicolas-Hays, Inc., 2012) that explores in depth many of the themes of this paper. Veronica is taking drawing classes, experimenting with memoir writing, and having jazz piano lessons. She is married to Robert Romanyshyn.

Robert Kugelmann. I am a professor of psychology at the University of Dallas. I began teaching here in 1982 at the invitation of Robert Romanyshyn, who was head of the department at that time. I am indebted to Robert for more than that! When I was looking into applying to grad schools in 1973, a friend of mine said, "Hey, have you heard about that new phenomenological program at Dallas?" No, I hadn't, but I looked into it. I caught the Greyhound from New York and came to Irving, when invited for an interview. That's when I met Robert Romanyshyn. He interviewed me in the cafeteria as we sipped cups of coffee from Styrofoam cups. I thought we had a great conversation and I hoped I'd get the chance to study with him. I did, and he was a reader of my dissertation some years later. We had some good arguments over that dissertation, but he was ever the insightful thinker, pushing me beyond the limits of my thinking. After I returned to the University in '82, I was blessed to have him as a colleague. It was a sad day in my life when he left UD, although I was happy to see his work so appreciated by Pacifica. His work has been an inspiration to me over the past four (!) decades.

Patrick Mahaffey, Ph.D., is a Core Faculty member and Associate Chair of the Mythological Studies Program at Pacifica Graduate Institute, a program he chaired for 18 years. As a religious studies scholar, his teaching and research focuses on Hindu and Buddhist traditions, comparative philosophy of religion, contemplative practices, and mysticism. He has conducted participant-observation research in India and practices Hindu and Buddhist forms of meditation. He has published essays on Hindu yoga traditions, Jung's depth psychology and yoga, religious pluralism, postmodernity, and religion in America.

Kareen Malone received her Ph.D. from the University of Dallas in psychology and literature. She studied phenomenological psychology at Duquesne University, phenomenology and humanistic psychology at Georgia State University and Jungian approaches and literature at the University of Dallas with Robert Romanyshyn and Thomas Moore. She has studied feminism & philosophy of Science, and Cognitive Science at the Georgia Institute of Technology. She is in analytic formation with Après Coup in Lacanian psychoanalysis New York. She studied with Groupe interdisciplinaire freudien de recherche et d'intervention clinique et culturelle in Quebec, Canada. She has co-edited three anthologies on Lacanian psychoanalysis, the most recent on Lacan and Addiction (Karnac Press, 2011). She co-authored a text *Science as Psychology* from Cambridge University Press. She is Co-Director of the Ph.D. program in Consciousness and Society. She is a fellow of the American Psychological Association and Past-President of The Society for Theoretical and Philosophical Psychology. She integrates Lacanian psychoanalysis and cultural studies with the goals of a more emancipatory psychology, clinical practice, and reflective discipline. She is Associate Editor of *Theory and Psychology*, and on the editorial board of *Psychoanalysis, Culture & Society and Subjectivity: International Journal of Critical Psychology*.

Stanton Marlan, Ph.D., ABPP, LP is a Jungian analyst and clinical psychologist in private practice in Pittsburgh, PA and a licensed psychoanalyst in the state of New York. He is an adjunct Clinical Professor of Psychology at Duquesne University, supervising graduate students at DU's psychology clinic. He is a training and supervising analyst with the Inter-Regional Society of Jungian Analysts, and is President of the Pittsburgh Society of Jungian Analysts. He holds diplomates in both clinical psychology and psychoanalysis from the American Board of Professional Psychology (ABPP) and is one of the Directors on The American Board and Academy of Psychoanalysis (ABApsa) He is on the advisory Board of Spring Journal Books, and on the editorial board of Jung Journal: Culture and Psyche. He is a past Editor of the Journal of Jungian Theory and Practice. He has published numerous articles on Jungian psychology and is the Editor of four books including *Archetypal Psychologies: Reflections in Honor of James Hillman*. He was a Fay lecturer at Texas A&M and is the author of *The Black Sun: The Alchemy and Art of Darkness*. Dr. Marlan has lectured widely at Jungian institutes and Archetypal conferences in the United States and abroad and has taught at the C.G. Jung Institute–

Zürich.

David L. Miller, Ph.D., is the Watson-Ledden Professor of Religion Emeritus at Syracuse University and a Core Faculty Person in Mythological Studies (retired) at Pacifica Graduate Institute. His teaching and research are in the areas of history of religion, comparative mythologies, literary theory, and depth psychology. Dr. Miller was a member of the Eranos Circle from 1975-1988, and he lectured at the Eranos Conferences in Ascona, Switzerland, nine times during this period. He is an honorary member of the Inter-Regional Society of Jungian Analysts, the International Association of Analytical Psychology, and the International Society for Psychology as the Discipline of Interiority. Dr. Miller is the author of more than one hundred articles and book chapters, and of five books, including *Gods and Games: Toward a Theology of Play; The New Polytheism: Rebirth of the Gods and Goddesses; Three Faces of God: Traces of the Trinity in Literature and Life; and, Hells and Holy Ghosts: A Theopoetics of Christian Belief.* See his website for more information: http://dlmiller.mysite.syr.edu/.

Rex Olson, Ph.D. is the director of Counseling Services at Alfred State College. After earning his BA (sociology) and teaching credentials from the University of California, Santa Barbara, he enjoyed a brief career as an elementary school teacher in Carlsbad, California. In 1978 he left California to pursue graduate studies in sociology at the University of North Carolina (Chapel Hill) and Syracuse University, being awarded the Master's degree from SU in 1981. His growing interest in metaphor and its relation to critical theory led him to the interdisciplinary study of rhetoric, depth psychology, and continental philosophy in the Humanities Doctoral Program at Syracuse University where he received his Ph.D. in 1994. In 2002 he was granted a second Ph.D. in clinical psychology from Duquesne University. Prior to his current appointment, Olson taught courses in general and existential-phenomenological psychology at Duquesne University, and introductory courses in sociology at Syracuse University and the University of North Carolina. He also has taught graduate courses in the Counseling Education Program and in the Community Services Administration Program, both at Alfred University.

Brent Dean Robbins, Ph.D., is Director of the Psychology Program and Associate Professor of Psychology at Point Park University in Pittsburgh,

PA. He has a doctorate in clinical psychology from Duquesne University, and is an outpatient therapist for Mercy Behavioral Health. He is President of the Society for Humanistic Psychology, and recipient of the Carmi Harari Early Career Award. He is editor-in-chief of the interdisciplinary journal, *Janus Head*, and editor of *Drugging Our Children: How Profiteers Are Pushing Antipsychotics on Our Youngest, and What We Can Do To Stop It* (Praeger, 2012).

David H. Rosen (a psychiatrist and Jungian psychoanalyst) was born in Port Chester, NY, and raised in New York, Texas, Missouri, and California. He earned his MD in 1970 from the University of Missouri. Dr. Rosen completed an internship at San Francisco General Hospital and did his psychiatric training at the Langley Porter Institute at the University of California, San Francisco, (UCSF). Since 1975 he has worked in academic medicine & psychiatry at UCSF, the University of Rochester (New York), and Texas A&M University. He was the first holder of the McMillan Professorship in Analytical Psychology at Texas A&M University (1986-2011). He continues to serve as the host and editor of the Annual Fay Lecture and Book Series in Analytical Psychology. Currently, Dr. Rosen is Affiliate Professor in Psychiatry at Oregon Health & Science University. Throughout his career, he has written eight books, including *Medicine as a Human Experience* with David Reiser (1984), *Evolution of the Psyche* with Michael Luebbert (1999), *The Tao of Jung: The Way of Integrity* (1997), *Transforming Depression: Healing the Soul Through Creativity* (3rd ed. 2002), and *The Healing Spirit of Haiku* with Joel Weishaus (2004). His other publications include articles, chapters, essays, and haiku poetry. Dr. Rosen maintains a long-standing interest in spirituality and the healing process. He has three daughters and two grandsons and currently lives with his wife, Lanara, and rescue dog, Willow, in Eugene, OR.

Susan Rowland, Ph.D., is Associate Chair of Hybrid Programs at Pacifica Graduate Institute and was previously Professor of English and Jungian Studies at the University of Greenwich, UK. She has published several books on literary theory, gender and depth psychology including *Jung: A Feminist Revision* (2002), *Jung as a Writer* (2005), *C.G. Jung in the Humanities* (2010). Her new book is *The Ecocritical Psyche: Literature, Complexity Evolution and Jung* (2012), arguing that literary symbols are embodied, biosemiotic and communicative between human and Other.

She is now working on a project on James Hillman and C.G. Jung as literary theorists together with another on goddesses in American women's detective fiction. She lives in California with her husband, digital literary artist, Joel Weishaus (rumors of her poetry have been greatly exaggerated). Susan was founding chair of the International Association of Jungian Studies 2003-6 and was program co-Chair with Dr John Beebe of the IAJS-IAAP joint academic conference in Zurich in 2008. When she called Dr Romanyshyn "the Ancient Mariner" to his face, he said he did not mind and Susan hopes this is so.

Ronald Schenk is a Jungian analyst, practicing and teaching in Dallas and Houston. He received his Master's Degree in Social Work from Washington University, St. Louis, and initial training in psychoanalytic psychotherapy in New Haven. He lived and worked with the Navajo Native Americans before receiving a Ph.D. in Psychology at the University of Dallas, in Phenomenological Psychology. He has written extensively in clinical and cultural psychology, and his most recent book is, *American Soul: A Cultural Narrative.*

Eva-Maria Simms is professor of psychology at Duquesne University in Pittsburgh. She is interested in philosophical psychology, particularly the phenomenology of children's experiences and the impact of nature, place, and community on children's lives. Her work includes *The child in the world: embodiment, time, and language in early childhood* (Detroit, Wayne State University Press, 2008) as well as publications on child development, Merleau-Ponty and phenomenology, language acquisition, eco-feminism, and a number of papers on the German poet Rilke and the scientific work of Goethe. Her qualitative research practice has as its goal the transformation of urban communities and their relationship to nature. She has taught in the US and in Germany, and is one of the founding editors of the literary publisher Autumn House Press. Address: simms@duq.edu

Michael P. Sipiora is a Core Faculty Member at Pacifica Graduate Institute where he teaches in the Clinical, Depth Psychology, and Mythological Studies programs. For over twenty years Sipiora was a professor at Duquesne University where he was an award winning teacher in their program in Human Science Psychology. Areas of his teaching and publication include phenomenological psychology and philosophy, archetypal psychology, and the rhetorical tradition. He earned a Bachelors and Masters in Philosophy at San Jose State University. His Masters and Doctorial studies in Psychology with a concentration in Literature were carried out at the University of Dallas. Sipiora is a licensed clinical psychologist who has practiced in both private and community mental health settings, and he has been active in narrative based, organizational development consulting.

Glen Slater, Ph.D., has studied and trained in religious studies and clinical psychology. For the past 15 years he has taught Jungian and archetypal psychology at Pacifica Graduate Institute. He edited and introduced the third volume of James Hillman's Uniform Edition, *Senex and Puer*, as well as a volume of essays by Pacifica faculty, *Varieties of Mythic Experience*, (with Dennis Patrick Slattery). Besides contributing to several Jungian essay collections, he writes regularly for the *Spring* journal, where he was for several years the film review editor. He divides his time between Bainbridge Island, Washington and Santa Barbara, California.

Dennis Patrick Slattery, Ph.D. has been teaching for 43 years, the last 18 in the Mythological Studies Program at Pacifica Graduate Institute in Carpinteria, California. He has authored, co-authored, edited and co-edited 17 books, including four volumes of poetry and one novel. His titles include: *The Idiot: Dostoevsky's Fantastic Prince* (1984); *The Wounded Body: Remembering the Markings of Flesh* (2000); *Grace in the Desert: Awakening to the Gifts of Monastic Life* (2004); *Harvesting Darkness: Essays on Myth, Film and Culture* (2006); with Glen Slater, co-edited *Varieties of Mythic Experience: Essays on Religion and Culture* (2008); With Charles Asher he co-authored *Simon's Crossing. A Novel* (2008); With Jennifer Selig he co-edited *Reimagining Education: Essays on Reviving the Soul of Learning* (2009); and *The Soul Does Not Specialize: Revaluing the Humanities and the Polyvalent Imagination*. His most recent book is *Riting Myth, Mythic Writing: Plotting Your Personal Story* (2012). Dr. Slattery offers Writing Retreats on Exploring One's Personal Myth, both in the United States and Europe.

Les Todres, Ph.D. Bournemouth University, United Kingdom, is a clinical psychologist and Professor of Health Philosophy at the School of Health and Social Care, Bournemouth University, U.K. Since the early 1970's he has been interested in the relationship between phenomenology, existentialism and hermeneutics. He took a descriptive phenomenological approach in both his masters thesis on the 'awareness of finitude' as well as in his PhD dissertation on the meaning of self-insight in psychotherapy. At the same time he was engaged in psychotherapeutic training, and through this was introduced to the Daseinsanalytic approach of Medard Boss, and thus to Martin Heidegger. His 2007 book, *Embodied Enquiry: phenomenological touchstones for research, psychotherapy and spirituality* (Palgrave Macmillan,) reflects a particular interest in the lived body as a way of knowing and being. Drawing particularly on the works of Merleau-Ponty and Gendlin he took qualitative research methodologies towards a more aesthetic emphasis, considered how psychotherapy addresses meanings carried in the body, and reflected on an embodied spirituality were the felt sense of a 'supportive mystery' is met in palpable way.

www.ingramcontent.com/pod-product-compliance
Lightning Source LLC
Chambersburg PA
CBHW030333270326
41926CB00010B/1605